THE MIRACULOUS LANGUAGE *of the* QUR'AN

Evidence of Divine Origin

BASSAM SAEH

INTERNATIONAL INSTITUTE OF ISLAMIC THOUGHT
LONDON • WASHINGTON

THE INTERNATIONAL INSTITUTE OF ISLAMIC THOUGHT
P.O. BOX 669, HERNDON, VA 22070, USA
www.iiit.org

LONDON OFFICE
P.O. BOX 126, RICHMOND, SURREY TW9 2UD, UK
www.iiituk.com

ISBN 978-1-56564-665-0

Cover design by Sideek Ali
Printed in Malta by Gutenberg Press

CONTENTS

Contents

FOREWORD

MUSLIMS ARE ENJOINED, along with the rest of humanity, to "read" and contemplate the message of the Qur'an and reflect on its origins as divine Revelation. In this fascinating study the author has endeavored to elucidate the many linguistically miraculous aspects of the sacred text, and why its beauty and perfection were utterly new and wondrous to the ears of 7th century Arabia, speechless with admiration on hearing its verses recited for the first time by the Prophet Muhammad (ṢAAS).* As masters of Arabic and so in a sense trained to hear and appreciate the Qur'an, their impression speaks volumes.

Yes, the Revelation is beautiful, in and of itself. But the Qur'an of course is so much more than this. Without exaggeration, the genius of its language, elegance, rhythm, rich imagery, fluidity, its weaving of metaphors and concepts, its many varied and previously unheard of styles and techniques of prose, as well as remarkable use of vocabulary, make it a work of eternal perfection. It immediately and powerfully impacted human intellect and behavior, spectacularly transforming the Arabic language, and bringing to the conscious of man a majestic vision, directing his attention to the highest things. It is some of these features that this work attempts to evoke and explain. The author has evidently given great thought to his subject matter, and his contribution focuses in essence on the question of what exactly makes the Qur'an linguistically miraculous?

This work is the English translation of the original Arabic abridged edition of the book entitled *Al-Muʿjizah*, volume 1, (IIIT, 2012). It is addressed to lay readers, so competence in Arabic is not essential to understand issues of morphology and other language technicalities

* (ṢAAS) – *Ṣallā Allāhu ʿalayhi wa sallam*: May the peace and blessings of God be upon him. Said whenever the name of the Prophet Muhammed is mentioned.

discussed, although ability to read Arabic would be beneficial, if not required. In attempting to unlock the secrets of its language and composition, Bassam Saeh guides readers to appreciate the beauty of the Qur'an, to become more immersed in it, and have a clearer understanding of its structure and flow. Devoting special attention to *Sūrah al-Muddaththir* (chapter 74) to underpin his analysis, he thus brings the Revelation to life, to demonstrate that each surah has distinct features and characteristics that make it stand out uniquely within the design and sweep of the whole.

No exposition is by itself sufficient for a full understanding of the Qur'an. But this work is an indispensable companion in the quest for a better comprehension of, and a closer affinity with, the sacred text. The translation used is mainly, *The Message of the Qur'an* by Muhammad Asad, with also *The Meaning of the Holy Qur'an* by Abdullah Yusuf Ali. Dates cited according to the Islamic calendar (hijrah) are labelled AH. Otherwise they follow the Gregorian calendar and labelled CE where necessary. Arabic words are italicized except for those which have entered common usage. Diacritical marks have been added only to those Arabic names not considered contemporary.

The IIIT, established in 1981, has served as a major center to facilitate serious scholarly efforts based on Islamic vision, values and principles. The Institute's programs of research, seminars and conferences during the last thirty years have resulted in the publication of more than four hundred and fifty titles in both English, Arabic and other major languages.

We express our thanks and gratitude to the author, Bassam Saeh, for his cooperation throughout the various stages of production. We are also grateful to the translator, Nancy Roberts, and the editorial and production team at the IIIT London Office and all those who were directly or indirectly involved in the completion of this publication.

IIIT LONDON OFFICE
May 2015

بسم الله الرحمن الرحيم

Of knowledge we have none, save what
You have taught us. (The Qur'an 2:32)

Preface

The Qur'an's Infallibility

The fact that the Qur'an is a literary masterpiece is beyond debate. The fact that it is a unique and matchless perfection of language, style, eloquence, and power, which the 7th century peoples of the Arabian peninsula had never encountered before, and have not encountered since, is also a matter beyond dispute. What is debated however is whether it is miraculous or not. In other words whether it is of this dimension or that of a divine other. Evidence of that divine authority is surfacing on multi-faceted and ever increasing levels of knowledge as humanity evolves and continues its centuries long assessment of the scripture. But for the purposes of this study, it is a particular element of the Qur'an's words, hitherto not fully grasped, which is brought to our attention attesting to the fact that it is a linguistic miracle of divine origin.

Differentiating Qur'anic language from human genius is another way of clearly stating that the Prophet was simply a channel to deliver God's final message, and that not even the most gifted minds, or those exceptionally talented in the arts of literature, oratory, and/or poetry, could produce a single chapter "like unto it" (10:38). This confident Qur'anic assertion to prove its statement false is note not only a wholly intellectual appeal and an open challenge to critics, drawing attention incidentally to the importance of deductive logic centuries ahead of its time, but also fantastic by the sheer simplicity with which it presents this greatest of challenges.

What has been the response? Two important facts with regards to the Qur'anic challenge have stood the test of time and remain a thorny problem for those who acknowledge its linguistic authority but cannot resolve its divine origins. These are integral to any debate but often conveniently overlooked by critics:

1. Not a single mistake, of any type, has been found in its over six thousand verses (not for lack of trying).
2. Despite many historical attempts at emulation, some in outright mockery of the Prophet, and others genuine by leading authorities in Arabic (keeping in mind the Prophet's era witnessed the finest exponents of the Arabic language the world has ever seen), to this day the whole exercise has been little more than utterly futile and embarrassing.

And we are not simply referring to language at this point because whether for the first time or after countless readings one would be hard put to define any one factor that makes the Qur'an utterly unique. One of the qualifications of the Qur'an's uniqueness is inimitability, and for the purposes of this study it is the inimitability of the Qur'an's language, marking one significant aspect of its divine authorship, and hence inherent miraculousness, which is analyzed – with the express understanding of course that language is being studied to gain a deeper appreciation of the Qur'an's core message. In essence the ideas, perspectives, and world the Qur'an plunges man into, and the heightened sense of moral virtue and sincere faith – the filters of self-appraisal through which it asks man to assess his actions and very motives by – are powerfully significant in terms of the alertness with which we are to understand our reality and place in the cosmos as well as the final Judgment which is to come once the illusion of this life and all physical existence passes away.

Throughout history, Muslim scholars have expounded on the aesthetic elements of the Qur'an's miraculous language as well as other literary factors, content, and astounding scientific verses. However, according to the author no one has tried to elucidate on what he terms a secret aspect of its language, something which due to familiarity with the Revelation we have given little thought to with the passage of time. And that secret is simply this: granted the Qur'an was revealed in the Arabic language, yet, at the same time it was an Arabic which was *new*, stunning the Arabs who first heard it. How it was new is the subject of this work.

Original and early Muslim audiences therefore responded to the Qur'an's words, sounds, rhythms etc. in a manner consistent with a deeper appreciation of its beauty and majesty. Something which our modern ears, soothed by familiarity, and despite being surrounded by all manner of dictionaries and studies, are often at a loss to capture. The author attempts to remove this veil somewhat and introduce readers to the Qur'an anew, with fresh eyes bringing to life something of this wonder.

Although the miraculous language of the Qur'an has been unquestionably accepted by Muslims, nevertheless a systematic study proving this belief through a methodical study of its language has to the best of the author's knowledge not yet been undertaken. Thus, he attempts to prove scientifically, and through comparison between the Qur'anic language on the one hand, and the language of pre-Islamic poetry, the Prophet's words (Hadith), and the language of the Arabs both past and present, on the other, that an important strand of the Qur'an's linguistic miraculousness is the fact that this Arabic was completely new.

The study attempts to empirically prove that the Arabs never knew this language before the Qur'an, and never could replicate it afterwards, while the language of the Prophet, despite its eloquence, was grasped and imitated, simply because it was first and foremost the language of a human being – one unfortunate outcome of this being the huge intermingling of genuine and forged Hadith. This has never happened to the Qur'an and will never happen to it, yet another testimony of the Qur'an being the word of God.

إِنَّا نَحْنُ نَزَّلْنَا الذِّكْرَ وَإِنَّا لَهُ لَحَافِظُونَ

Lo! We, even We, reveal the Reminder, and lo!
We verily are its Guardian. (15:9)

IIIT LONDON OFFICE

The Miraculous Language of the Qur'an

Evidence of Divine Origin

INTRODUCTION

IT ALL BEGAN IN 1989 when the Oxford Centre for Islamic Studies asked me to present a number of lectures to British students seeking a better understanding of the Arabic language through the Holy Qur'an. After trying to translate the meanings of the Qur'an into English for my students, I found myself drawn by their challenging questions beyond the boundaries of the linguistic traditions and conventions familiar to interpreters and linguists.

At the time I just happened to be editing a book written in the Andalusian period with a British Orientalist and friend at Oxford University's The Oriental Institute. One day my friend asked me, "Which is correct in Arabic: *mā zāla* (مازال) or *lā zāla* (لازال)?" Without giving it much thought, I replied, "*Mā zāla*." After some discussion, however, he insisted that *lā zāla* was correct, while I insisted on *mā zāla*. In the end he surprised me by saying, "Well, then, either you're mistaken, or God is! After all, the Qur'an only uses *lā zāla*!"

For a moment I was speechless. Then I gathered my wits and asked him in turn, "So how would you translate the verb *kāna* (كان) into English?" "Was," he replied without hesitation. "If that's the case," I continued, "then how would you translate the following phrase from the Qur'an: *wa kāna Allāhu ghafūran raḥīmā* وكان الله غفوراً رحيما?" "And God is Oft-Forgiving, Most Merciful." He replied as confidently as before. "Where is the verb *kāna* in this translation?" I wanted to know. But he couldn't answer me, since the only verb one can use to translate this statement is "is," which would be equivalent to *yakūnu* (يكون) or *inna* (إنّ) in Arabic, but not the past tense verbal form *kāna* (كان) .

The Qur'an has unique language and linguistic uses that differ from our human uses of language, both formal and informal. No one, even the Prophet Muhammad himself, has ever used the past tense verb *kāna* in the sense of "is." However, this very usage occurs 190 times in the Qur'an. When I went back to the Qur'an to verify what my Orientalist friend had said about *mā zāla*, I was surprised to find that what he had said was not accurate, and that the Qur'an uses the negative particle *mā* (ما)only with the past tense, that is, *mā zāla* (مازال) and the negative particle *lā* (لا)only with the present tense, as in the phrase *lā yazālu* (لايزال). Hence, we find neither *lā zāla* (لازال) nor *mā yazālu* (مايزال) anywhere in the Qur'an. However, the greatest surprise I encountered was the ways in which Qur'anic uses of the verb, in both its past (*zāla* - زال) and present (*yazālu* - يزال) forms, differ from our human uses of it. When we say, *mā zāla al-maṭaru yahṭulu*, which means literally, "the rain has not ceased to fall," the listener understands this statement to mean that it was raining earlier and that it is still raining now. The use of the expression *mā zāla* thus conveys a meaning that spans the past and the present, but not the future. This is the commonly accepted human usage of this verb. However, the past tense phrase *mā zāla* in the only two Qur'anic verses in which it occurs includes the past only. In other words, it conveys the sense of something continuing in the past, but without its having continued into the present. The verses are as follows:

فما زالت تلك دعواهم حتى جعلناهم حصيداً خامدين (الأنبياء:١٥)

And that cry of theirs did not cease (*mā zālat tilka daʿwāhum*) until We caused them to become [like] a field mown down, still and silent as ashes. (*Sūrah al-Anbiyā'* 21:15)

ولقد جاءكم يوسفُ من قبلُ بالبيّناتِ فما زلتُم في شكٍّ ممّا جاءكم به حتّى إذا هلكَ قلتُم لن يَبعثَ اللهُ من بعدِه رسولاً (غافر:٣٤)

> ...it was to you that Joseph came aforetime with all evidence of the truth; but you never ceased to throw doubt on all [the messages] that he brought you (*mā ziltum fī shakkin mimmā jā'akum bihi*)—so much so that when he died, you said, "Never will God send any apostle [even] after him!" (*Sūrah Ghāfir* 40:34)

The first of these two verses means that the people continued to cry out until they were destroyed, all of which took place in the past, while the second means that the people of Joseph's time clung to their doubts concerning his message until he died. This, too, took place entirely in the past. In both these cases, the action concerned began and ended in the past, and did not extend into the realm of the present.

As for the Qur'anic use of the present-tense phrase *lā yazālu*, it includes the past, the present, and the future. Whatever action is being referred to was done in the past, is still being done in the present, and will continue to be done in the future. This semantic phenomenon is observable in the following three verses:

ولا يزالون يقاتلونكم حتىّ يردّوكم عن دينِكم (البقرة:٢١٧)

> [Your enemies] will not cease to fight against you (*lā yazālūna yuqātilūnakum*) till they have turned you away from the faith, if they can. (*Sūrah al-Baqarah* 2:217)

لا يزالُ بُنيانُهمُ الذي بَنَوا رِيبَةً في قلوبِهم إلاّ أنْ تَقَطَّعَ قلوبُهم (التوبة:١١٠)

> The building which they have built will never cease to be (*lā yazālu bunyānuhum alladhī banaw*) a source of disquiet in their hearts until their hearts crumble to pieces. (*Sūrah al-Tawbah* 9:110)

ولو شاء ربُّكَ لجعلَ الناسَ أمّةً واحدةً ولا يزالون مختلفِين. إلاّ من رحِمَ ربُّك

(هود:١١٨–١١٩)

> And had thy Sustainer so willed, He could surely have made all mankind one single community: but [He willed it otherwise, and so] they continue to hold divergent views (*wa lā yazālūna mukhtalifīn*)—[all of them], save those upon whom they Sustainer has bestowed His grace. (*Sūrah Hūd* 11:118-119)

The intellectual encounters with the Other taking place in the modern Western world are what first sparked my decision to reexamine my usual reading of the Qur'an. This reading of mine had been numbed by the perilous effect of familiarity and daily repetition, which blind us to much of what was experienced and understood by the Arabs of the Prophet's day when they received the first verses that had begun descending in succession on the Messenger of God. These early recipients of the Qur'an were shocked and bewildered by its newness, since in it they found a style that departed from everything they were familiar with. This shock and bewilderment then turned into critical questions: What's happening around me? Whatever it was, it had to be too far-reaching and critical to be nothing but the distinctive style of an emerging writer, a poet on the rise, or a would-be prognosticator.

In Volume One of this book I attempt to introduce readers to these Qur'anic secrets as gently and deliberately as possible. In so doing, I highlight the changes the Qur'an introduced into the linguistic framework of the Arabic language, prefacing each new element with a detailed explanation of its nature and types. Textual support is taken from various surahs of the Qur'an, with special attention being devoted to *Sūrah al-Muddaththir*, one of the earliest surahs, and the ways in which it clashed with Arabic linguistic conventions. Most chapters in this section partly deal with the newly emerging linguistic, grammatical and rhetorical aspects of this surah.

In Volume Two, I apply the phenomena discussed in Volume One to each individual surah of the Qur'an. I begin with the shortest, most frequently recited surah, namely, *Sūrah al-Fātiḥah* (1). I then deal with the last twenty surahs, beginning with *Sūrah al-Nās* (114), *Sūrah al-Falaq* (113), *Sūrah al-Ikhlāṣ* (112), and so on, moving back to *Sūrah al-Tīn* (95).

Despite the undoubtedly pioneering nature of the work we are embarking on, unrestrained by the longstanding tendency to obfuscate the true nature of the linguistic innovation that characterizes the Qur'an, the discerning researcher should never lose sight of the fact that no matter what objective forms or approaches it takes, any human interpretation or linguistic analysis of the Qur'an and any disclosure of its miraculousness, be it in the realm of rhetoric, language or science, is a process of weighing probabilities that necessarily remains subject to the possibilities of human error. Hence, everything we propose in this connection is no more than a sincere attempt to approach the absolute truth which, ultimately, we find ourselves incapable of reaching as long as we are dealing with the infinite, the divine, and the miraculous armed with nothing but our weak and limited capacities.

MIRACLE, OR MERE GENIUS?

All my life I have had a firm belief in the miraculousness of the language of the Qur'an. In the beginning I held this belief simply by virtue of being a Muslim even though, in actuality, I was unable to appreciate this miraculousness with my reason; I lacked the capacity to discern it clearly with the primitive means of research at my disposal. However, in the language of the Qur'an I saw captivating beauty, boundless expressiveness, eloquence, rhythm, magic and distinction. What I failed to realize was that these qualities are one thing, and that miraculousness is something else – something more profound, more unattainable, more subtle, and more beyond human reach. I had always indulged in the hope that, once I had gained a proper grasp of Arabic rhetoric, I would be able to identify the miraculousness in the Qur'an that none of the books I had read had been able to demonstrate for me in a scientific, irrefutable manner.

The authors of such books had of course used the word "miraculousness" (*i*ʿ*jāz*) in their titles. However, all these books had talked about was the Qur'an's eloquence, splendor, beauty, and precision of expression. All of these are features that we might find, to one degree or another, in works of literature produced in various languages and by various peoples of the world. One can easily think of numerous geniuses who have held the world spellbound with their literary, intellectual and artistic creations. But whatever description such creations might merit, none of them can rightly be described as miraculous. Why, then, do we insist on singling out the Qur'an alone for this description? And where is the miraculousness in the Qur'an if miraculousness is defined as that which surpasses human capacity? Taken all together, the various features of these noble creations might well border on the miraculous. However, even these would not be sufficient to demonstrate, in irrefutable scientific fashion, the miraculousness whose existence we hope to discover and demonstrate.

Later in my life, after graduating with a Bachelor's Degree in Arabic, I was faced with the same unanswered question. I then completed a Masters Degree, followed by a Ph.D. in Arabic Literature. Again, however, I still found myself unable to see the miraculous aspect of the language of the Qur'an despite the fact that, from my own perspective, at least, I had become literary researcher and critic well practiced in the arts of language and literature.

As I searched for the basis of my faith in the Qur'an's miraculousness, I was constantly faced by a methodological dilemma, namely, how to reconcile within myself the Muslim and the researcher. Or, more simply put, how was I to reconcile religious sentiment with its capacity for give and take and my inborn faith in the miraculous nature of the Qur'an and the truth of Islam and its scripture, with airtight, abstract scientific analysis whose verdicts are unaffected by emotion, faith, individual interpretations or preconceptions? Where lie the nebulous, elusive boundaries between human genius on one hand, and on the other hand, divine miracle proven by scientific facts and figures the verdicts associated with which have nothing to do with personal preferences, changeable human attitudes, conjectures, probabilities and expectations?

Then came the third phase of my academic life, when I came face to face with the urgent and bewildering question: Wherein lies the miraculousness (*iʿjāz*) of the Qur'an's language? In posing this question, I used the word "miraculousness" in its true, original sense, not merely in the sense of genius, eloquence, distinction, precision and beauty. I began to wonder whether the word "miraculousness" had lost its real significance for us, having reverted to being nothing but some term whose original significance we no longer recalled or recognized, and which no longer meant anything to us but superiority, excellence, or brilliance.

WHAT DID THE TERM *IʿJĀZ* (MIRACULOUS) MEAN TO EARLY ISLAMIC THINKERS?

Muslim scholars from both earlier and later periods undertook thorough and tireless studies of what they referred to as the miraculousness of the Qur'an (*iʿjāz al-Qur'ān*). Such studies dealt with three main areas:

1. ***The aesthetic or rhetorical aspect of the Qur'an:*** Studies dealing with this aspect of the Qur'an's language set out to demonstrate that the Qur'an is an aesthetic miracle in its language and arrangement. The first scholars to develop this theme include al-Jāḥiẓ (255 AH/869 CE), Abū al-Ḥasan ʿAlī al-Rummānī (374 AH/984 CE), Muḥammad Ibn Yazīd al-Wāsiṭī (306 AH/918 CE), Abū Zayd al-Balkhī (323 AH/934 CE), Abū Hilāl al-ʿAskarī (395 AH/1005 CE), al-Khaṭṭābī (378

AH/988 CE), Abū Bakr Muḥammad ibn al-Ṭayyib al-Bāqillānī (404 AH/1013 CE), al-Qāḍī ʿAbd al-Jabbār al-Asadābādī (416 AH/1025 CE), ʿAbd al-Qāhir al-Jurjānī (474 AH/1078 CE), Ibn Abī al-Iṣbaʿ (654 AH/1256 CE), Ibn al-Qayyim al-Jawziyyah (751 AH/1350 CE), and others. However, beauty remains a relative phenomenon which, as such, is subject to debate, and the standards relevant to which may differ from one individual to another, one society to another, and one era to another. Hence, it needs to be recognized that if virtually any Western, non-Muslim linguist adopted the same approaches and methods adhered to by Muslim scholars in their study of the Qur'an, he would be led to conclude that geniuses the likes of Shakespeare, Dante, Rousseau and Goethe were also gods.

2. ***The expressional aspect*:** Studies dealing with the Qur'an's expressional dimension aim to show that the Qur'an is a linguistic miracle based on its precision of expression. Authors of such studies discuss the subtle distinctions among Qur'anic terms, structures and expressions which, although they appear to be alike, are not actually so. Such terms, structures and expressions, which came to be known among scholars as *mutashābih al-Qur'ān*, were pointed out by al-Jāḥiẓ in his book *al-Bayān wa al-Tabyīn*. Reference was also made to them by al-Qāḍī ʿAbd al-Jabbār in his book, *Mutashābih al-Qur'ān*, by Muḥammad ibn ʿAbd Allāh al-Iskāfī (d. 420 AH/1029 CE) in his book entitled *Durrat al-Tanzīl wa Ghurrat al-Ta'wīl*, by Fakhr al-Dīn al-Rāzī (d. 606 AH/1209 CE) in *Asrār al-Tanzīl*, by Maḥmūd ibn Ḥamzah al-Kirmānī (d. 505 AH/1111 CE) in *Al-Burhān fī Tawjīh Mutashābih al-Qur'ān*, and others.

3. ***The scientific aspect*:** Contrary to popularly held belief, this theme began to appear quite early in the written Islamic tradition. Early Islamic scholars, and later scholars as well, attempted to demonstrate the miraculous nature of the Qur'an based on the fact that it speaks of cosmic realities and natural phenomena that were not discovered

until long after the appearance of the Qur'an itself. If these writings weren't so haphazard and unscientific, they would be virtually unassailable. Unfortunately, however, most of the contemporary scholars who have treated this theme have done little more than made fools of both themselves and their readers. They demonstrate no specialized knowledge of the miraculousness they purport to demonstrate, nor do they present their case in an academic fashion, since their writings are devoid of any documentation or quotations from Western scholarly writings and research relating to the scientific phenomena being referred to. Early scholars could be excused to a great extent for their failure to make reference to such sources, and they were actually more systematic than their modern counterparts. Early Muslim thinkers had mastered the scientific disciplines and discoveries of their day. In fact, they were the primary authorities on such matters, as human civilization at that time was being written from right to left. Muslims spoke, and the world listened. The Muslim world dictated, and the rest of the world wrote. Today, by contrast, things are precisely the opposite. The centers of academic and scientific research, discovery, innovation and decision-making have moved to the other side of the world, and civilization is being written from left to right. The first Muslim scholars to write on the theme of "scientific miraculousness" (*al-iʿjāz al-ʿilmī*) were al-Jāḥiẓ, Ibn Surāqah (d. 415 AH/1023 CE), al-Māwardī (d. 450 AH/1058 CE), al-Ghazālī (d. 505 AH/1111 CE), al-Qāḍī ʿIyāḍ (d. 544 AH/1149 CE), Fakhr al-Dīn al-Rāzi, Ibn Abī al-Faḍl al-Mursī (d. 655 AH/1257 CE), and Dāwūd al-Anṭākī (d. 1008 AH/1599 CE). Later Muslim writers to take up this theme include al-Iskandarānī (d. 1307 AH/1889 CE), Abd al-Rahman al-Kawakibi (d. 1320 AH/1903 CE), and Tantawi Jawhari (d. 1359 AH/1940 CE). The writing movement on this topic picked up speed in the twentieth century, resulting in the publication of a series of books dealing with what has been termed the numerical miraculousness (*al-iʿjāz al-ʿadadī*) of the Qur'an. One of the earliest books in this category was *Al-Iʿjāz al-ʿAdadī fī al-Qur'ān al-Karīm* by Abd al-Razzaq Nawfal, which came out in the early 1970s. In his book, Nawfal includes long lists of the "pairings" (*al-mathānī*) on which the language of the Qur'an is based. We find, for example, that the words meaning "night" (*layl*) and "day" (*nahār*) occur the same number of times in the Qur'an. Similarly, the words referring to paradise (*al-jannah*) and hell (*al-nār*) occur equal numbers of times, and words referring to angels (*malā'ikah*) and demons (*shayāṭīn*) occur equal numbers of times. He even notes that the word for "month" (*shahr*) occurs exactly twelve times in the Qur'an, while the word for "day" (*yawm*) occurs exactly 365 times. Fakhr al-Dīn al-Rāzi was the first to draw attention to this linguistic mystery in the Qur'an in the context of discussing the term *mathāni* in *Sūrah al-Zumar* 39:23, which speaks of the Qur'an as "a divine writ fully consistent within itself (*kitāban mutashābihan*), repeating each statement [of the truth] in manifold forms (*mathāniya*) – [a divine writ] whereat shiver the skins of all who of their Sustainer stand in awe..."[1]

As for this book, it will focus exclusively on what I consider to be the truly miraculous aspect of the language of the Qur'an, namely, its newness. It is a newness that is not limited to a word here or an expression there. Rather, it encompasses the language of the entire Qur'an from beginning to end: vertically and horizontally, linguistically and rhetorically, on the level of words, particles, structures, and expressions; in terms of formulations, rhythms, images, and explanations, and with an intensity the likes of which no human being could have produced or even approached. Yet despite this linguistic newness the Qur'an preserved the foundations of the Arabic language and was eminently comprehensible to the people who heard it. Indeed, not only did they understand the Qur'an despite the newness of its language; they were unspeakably impressed by it.

THE IMPACT OF THE QUR'AN'S NEWNESS ON THE ARABS OF THE PROPHET'S DAY

The newness of the Qur'an, which manifested itself on the various levels of both content and style – from word choice, to expression, grammar, morphology, and rhetoric – was a source of perplexity and amazement to those who heard the revelation for the first time. A simple, three-word Qur'anic phrase such as *faṣdaᶜ bi mā tu'mar* ("Hence, proclaim openly all that thou hast been bidden [to say]" – *Sūrah al-Ḥijr* 15:94) prompted a certain Bedouin Arab to exclaim, "What is this that I hear? This is no merely human speech!" Then he prostrated himself with the words, "So eloquent was this speech that I bowed down in worship to the one who said that."[2]

Something subtle and mysterious is taking place here which our modern ears are unable to discern. How can we listen with the ear of ᶜUmar ibn al-Khaṭṭāb or the Bedouin Arab referred to above, or with the ears of other Arabs who surrendered their wills to God the moment they heard the language of the Holy Qur'an? If we could somehow replace our ears with theirs, might we discern the same miraculous quality that they did? Might we experience through its language what they experienced, and grasp what we have heretofore been unable to put our fingers on?

I always used to wonder myself how the Qur'an could challenge the Arabs of its day to produce something like it. Such a challenge was provocative, but it was also realistic and reasonable. For it then to challenge them to produce only ten surahs like it was astounding and even a bit disturbing, being a powerful and extraordinary sign of the confidence of the party making the challenge. But for it then to challenge them – not once, but twice, in two different surahs which were revealed at very different times (*Sūrah al-Baqarah* 2:23 and *Sūrah Yūnus* 10:38) – to produce a single surah like it was more than extraordinary. It signaled far more than the usual confidence of someone making a dare. What if they had actually risen to the challenge? What if their leading poets, litterateurs, orators, linguists and geniuses had joined forces to write a single small surah the length of *Sūrah al-Ḍuḥā* (93), or perhaps even the length of *Sūrah al-ʿAṣr* (103) or *Sūrah al-Kawthar* (108)? It would only have been a matter of composing a single line, no more! Would this have been so taxing for them? Wasn't the Qur'an in their own language, and weren't they masters of that very language?

THE TRUE EXTENT OF THE MIRACULOUSNESS MANIFESTED IN THE QUR'AN'S LINGUISTIC NEWNESS

When I set out to answer these questions by bringing the language of the Qur'an into my linguistic laboratory and placing its fabric under the microscope, I had no real conception of the type of challenge I had set myself. Never before had I realized, with complete confidence and clarity, that behind every verse, behind every expression – and I might almost say, behind every word – of the Qur'an there lies a miracle, or an "invention," nay, more than a single invention in many cases. It distressed me that I could not seem to find anything better than this inadequate human term to describe a miracle that human language cannot contain. After all, "God's is the loftiest likeness."[3] So I bowed my head in awe at the lofty wisdom that lay concealed in this divine dare.

I find that whenever I approach the language of the Qur'an in an attempt to unearth its secrets, I feel like a pygmy trying to scale the toe of an enormous giant. What we find in this language is not a scientific invention of the sort we witness in our day and age. Rather it consists of an ongoing series of astonishing linguistic innovations with a variety of features and forms. They are linked to another in such a way that whoever attempts to imitate them comes up against an impenetrable wall, and he/she realizes there is no place for arrogance or self-importance.

Suppose you had a beautiful garden where you spent time every day, smelling a flower here, discovering a new bud there, and picking fruits from this tree or that. And suppose someone came and told you that in the garden you enjoy every day and where you regularly see untold objects of beauty, there were thousands of amazing secrets you had never laid eyes on even though they were right under your nose. Further, suppose this person offered to give you glasses that would open your eyes to a scene entirely different from what you'd been accustomed to seeing in the past such that now, under every rock in the garden you found a precious pearl, between every couple of rose leaves a delicate sheet of silver, beneath the bark of every tree a sap made of a sublime perfume, and between every couple of specks of dust a particle of precious metal. Suppose you discovered that all this had been in your garden without your knowing a thing about it!

The better part of the work I did in preparation for writing this book consisted in looking for those special glasses. And once I'd found them, I determined to take fellow readers of the Qur'an by the hand so that, by donning these new glasses themselves, they could free themselves from the deadly familiarity that had destroyed their ability to see the boundless, mysterious miracles of language that had lain so long before their very eyes and of which they had not known a thing.

THE MIRACULOUS FREQUENCY OF QUR'ANIC INNOVATIONS

I remember once seeing a picture riddle that consisted of a photograph of what looked like strange, towering mountain chains. There was such an awe-inspiring, eerie quality about it that it seemed to have been taken of the surface of the moon or Mars. When I turned the piece of paper over to find out what the picture represented, I learned to my surprise that it was nothing but a highly magnified picture of the delicate lines that make up a human fingerprint. This, I suspect, is the kind of feeling readers will experience when they see the contours of the language of the Qur'an, or what we have managed to discover of them thus far, through the magnifying glass with which this study aims to supply them. With the help of this device, readers can at last catch a glimpse of the Qur'an's dazzling linguistic phenomena in all their bewildering glory.

If we looked at one of these phenomena in isolation from those that precede or follow it, we might be tempted to withhold judgment, thinking to ourselves: it is certainly innovative. But since when was innovation a miracle? And we would be right to raise such an objection, because, in fact, there would be no justification for claiming that the Qur'an is miraculous based on nothing but one, two or even three isolated cases. However, when we discover the density and frequency of the innovative phenomena that run through the Qur'an's verses and surahs; when we see how one follows on the other nonstop – in a single breath, without breaks or gaps of any kind; and when we see how every word, structure and expression in the Qur'an conceals wonders of expressive innovation of all colors and shapes, we begin to perceive the true linguistic miraculousness of the Qur'an and the impossibility of mimicking or forging it.

Someone might ask: Is there anything in the world that can't be counterfeited anymore? People have managed to counterfeit the US dollar, the British sterling pound, the Euro, and most, and if not all, of the world's other currencies as well. They have produced imitations of statues, literary works, ancient columns and coins, and paintings of the greatest and best-known artists in the world. So why couldn't someone write one or two surahs or verses like those in the Qur'an? However, it would be one thing to imitate something so successfully that people failed to detect the forgery, at least in the beginning, and, once the forgery had been discovered, for them to punish you as you deserved while secretly admiring you for the way you had mastered your craft. But it would be another thing to forge something and for people's response to be nothing but mockery, disdain, and accusations of ignorance and frivolity. And it is this latter scenario that has faced everyone who has ever set out to imitate the language of the Qur'an.

THE PERPLEXING EFFECT OF THE NEW RHYTHMIC STRUCTURE ON THE QUR'AN'S ARAB LISTENERS

To the primitive Bedouin Arabs who lived in the days of the Prophet Muhammad, the revelation of the Qur'an was comparable to the descent of a huge flying saucer before their very eyes: strange, sophisticated, masterfully crafted. Like people the world over, the Arabs of that day did not generally accept a new expressional form, be it poetry or prose, until their ears had grown accustomed to its distinctive rhythm, style and structures over several generations. If a writer, orator and poet departed from such familiar forms, listeners would hear nothing but a painful dissonance until, after it had been repeated in their hearing over a number of years, it became a recognized part of their linguistic repertoire.

Remarkably, however, they did not experience this kind of dissonance when they were confronted for the first time with the huge throngs of verbal, grammatical and expressional newcomers in the Qur'an. With their unique, recurring assemblages, these newly appearing linguistic phenomena were destined to build their own distinctive rhythmic repertoire in their listeners' ears, hearts, and minds within an unprecedentedly short period of time. Contrary to what one would expect, what drew the Arabs of the Prophet's day to the Qur'an from the moment they first encountered it was the rhythm and music of its language, which included both the sounds produced by the recitation, and the emotions and associations aroused by the images and meanings it conveyed. Despite being entirely new to the Arabs, this new rhythm and cadence were nevertheless acceptable and even welcomed, though they were perplexing even to the most eloquent and literarily versed polytheists. It was this latter group who, when they heard the Qur'an, couldn't help but voice their admiration for it despite their unbelief. Despite his refusal to enter Islam, al-Walīd ibn al-Mughīrah, a leading polytheist of that day, spoke highly of the Qur'an, saying:

> I swear by God, there isn't a man among you more knowledgeable than I of poetry or more able to distinguish bad verse from good. Nay, there is no one among you more knowledgeable than I of the poetry of the jinn themselves! Nevertheless, I swear by God, what this man is saying bears no resemblance to the poetry of either human beings or the jinn. His words have a sweetness about them, a beauty and an elegance. [Like a towering tree], they bear fruit from above, and their roots plunge deep. They rise above those around them, and none can rise above them.[4]

A MACHINE TO TRANSPORT ME BACK IN TIME

Time and time again I wondered to myself whether there was some sort of machine that could carry me back fourteen centuries so that I could hear the Qur'an through the ears of the seventh-century desert Arabs who were being exposed to the Qur'an for the very first time. Would it be possible for me, I wondered, to strip myself of my Qur'anic memory, and even my Islamic memory, so as to become a pre-Islamic Arab living in the age of the Qur'anic revelation? If so, I would listen to the Qur'an as it was being revealed, verse by verse, with pristine ears that hadn't yet heard the Qur'an so repeatedly that its very familiarity now prevented me from perceiving its genius, newness and uniqueness. What a marvelous experience it must have been for the seventh-century Muslims who received the revelation from God Himself for the very first time! How exhilarating it must have been for them to hear the Divine's authoritative, unquestionable pronouncements "live and on the air" on all their practical concerns: pronouncements that might entail acquittal or condemnation, promise or threat for people among whom they lived their daily lives. What must it have been like for them to hear what God had to say when the divine speech ushered them daily, even hourly, into worlds so vast that their minds could hardly contain them?

Try with me to envisage what sort of an impact the following verses would have had on the mind of the seventh-century Arabs who were hearing them for the first time:

> And no true understanding of God have they [who worship aught beside Him], inasmuch as the whole of the earth will be as a [mere] handful to Him on Resurrection Day, and the heavens will be rolled up in His right hand: limitless is He in His glory, and sublimely exalted above anything to which they may ascribe a share in His divinity! And [on that Day,] the trumpet [of judgment] will be sounded, and all [creatures] that are in the heavens and all that are on earth will fall down senseless, unless they be such as God wills [to exempt]. And then it will sound again – and lo! standing [before the Seat of Judgment], they will begin to see [the truth]! And the earth will shine bright with her Sustainer's light. And the record [of everyone's deeds] will be laid bare, and all the prophets will be brought forward, and all [other] witnesses; and judgment will be passed on them all in justice. And they will not be wronged. (*Sūrah al-Zumar* 39:67-69)

Now, fourteen centuries since these verses were revealed you may not perceive anything but the earth-shaking message they convey, a message that would have stretched the imaginations of seventh-century Arabs – and non-Arabs as well, perhaps – beyond their limits. How much more challenging it would have been, then, if this message was revealed in a new, dazzling garb, clad in a bewildering array of new linguistic forms with which no Arab would have been familiar at that time, and with such intensity that their minds would have been unable to take it in? Is it possible for us to recover those luminous moments that released such power, strength, faith, confidence and determination in the minds and hearts of the first Muslims that they were able to build a civilization that changed the course of history?

Pre-Islamic poetry and the Prophetic hadiths are the only two confirmed sources on the basis of which we can reconstruct the language that was contemporary with that of the Qur'an. Hence, in an attempt to recover those luminous moments of which I've spoken above, I decided to remove the Qur'anic memory from my brain's hard drive and replace it, first with the poetic memory of the pre-Islamic Arab, and then with the memory of the Prophetic hadiths.

THREE VOCABULARIES: QUR'ANIC, PRE-ISLAMIC, AND PROPHETIC

In my attempts to identify the stylistic differences between the Holy Qur'an and both pre-Islamic poetry and the Prophetic hadiths, I chose to focus on poetry in particular. The electronic encyclopedias available to us have thus far counted up some twenty thousand verses of pre-Islamic poetry. This number of verses is equal to, or slightly larger than, the size of the Qur'an, although we know that the amount of pre-Islamic poetry that has been lost may be even greater than that which has survived.[5]

Pre-Islamic poetry has a special linguistic quality that is easily distinguishable from the language of the Prophet even though he was born and lived in the heart of the pre-Islamic period. Similarly, the Prophet Muhammad had a special linguistic style that was entirely distinguishable from the language of the book which he brought to us. Moreover, these three languages never mixed in the least. These facts serve as clear evidence of the reliability of the texts that have come down to us in these three linguistic styles, not one of which has infiltrated or overlapped with either of the other two. By contrast, one finds that the styles of the pre-Islamic poets often resemble one another and overlap to such an extent that those who study them find it impossible to draw an unqualified, clear-cut distinction between one pre-Islamic poet and another based on their styles and linguistic persona. Even though these poets differ from each other in terms of strength or weakness, purity of style, delicacy, simplicity, abstruseness, and the like, no literary critic would dare to state with absolute certainty that such-and-such a poem was composed by a particular pre-Islamic poet rather than another, whereas even an ordinary reader of the Qur'an would be able to say with certainty that such-and-such a phrase or passage is from the Qur'an, while another is not.

Despite the fact that the language of the Prophetic hadiths, that is, the language used by the Prophet himself, must have been influenced, however superficially, by that of the Qur'an, this influence is hardly in evidence in more than one percent of the entire Hadith corpus. Nor does this influence alter the fundamental character of the Hadith literature. Hence, I have sought in the course of this study to identify the widespread and radical stylistic and linguistic differences between the Prophetic hadiths and the Qur'an in the hope of highlighting them for Orientalists and skeptics who have cast doubt on the divine origin of the Qur'an and accused the Apostle Muhammad and/or his contemporaries of forging it.

THE NEW LINGUISTIC REVOLUTION

How did the Arabs of the Prophet's day receive the new language found in the Holy Qur'an when it contained none of the idioms, phrases and constructions with which they had been familiar up to that time? In short, it left them at a loss. In fact, it may have left them in a state of shock that only began wearing off after some time had passed and they had gained some familiarity with this new language.

The linguistic shift of which I speak was not limited to the vocabulary of the Qur'an. Rather, it went beyond the level of individual words to the relationships among words, their placement within their various contexts, their uses, and the new linguistic, grammatical and imaginal elements and conventions that governed and permeated its language. The shift likewise encompassed the linguistic units that were ultimately formed from these individual words, relationships, and conventions. When we examine each surah of the Qur'an individually, we discover that the locations where new linguistic phenomena occur outnumber the words in the surah itself. In a surah as short as the *al-Fātiḥah* (1), which consists of 29 words, there are no fewer than 58 of these "new developments." In *Sūrah al-Nās* (114), which is 20 words long, we find no fewer than 33 new phenomena; in *Sūrah al-Falaq* (113) (23 words long), 38 new phenomena appear; and in *Sūrah al-Ikhlāṣ* (112) (15 words long), there are as many as 22 new phenomena. And a similar pattern is observable in all other surahs as well. Bearing this in mind, we can begin to imagine the magnitude of the shock which the Qur'an, with its matchless linguistic character, produced in the minds and hearts of seventh-century Arabs of the Arabian Peninsula.

The Qur'an most certainly did not bring a new language separate from the Arabic language that was already in existence. And it is in precisely this in which its miraculousness consists. The Qur'an was revealed in the Arabic language and remained rooted on its foundations. However, its uniqueness inheres in the way in which it went beyond the existing Arabic language, surpassing the limitations of its terms, structures, idioms, formulations, images and internal relationships. The miraculousness of the Qur'an consists in the way in which it developed the Arabic language's conventions and rules yet without abolishing them, thereby opening the way for it to evolve and grow richer, and endowing it with dimensions and horizons the breadth of which its speakers had never dreamed of.

The miraculousness of the Qur'an does not consist in its having created a language out of nothing. If it had done this, it would have separated itself and its teachings from all human beings, whatever their language. Rather, its miraculousness consists in its having constructed a new language on the very foundations of the old language, then gone soaring through vast realms that the traditional language had never known or accessed. During my lectures on the topic of this study, my listeners have often objected to my use of the term "new language" to refer to the language of the Qur'an, since this phrase might give the mistaken impression that the language of the Qur'an is something other than Arabic, and they have suggested that I use some alternative expression. However, the miraculousness of the Qur'an lies in this very paradox: the paradox of its being truly Arabic, and its being, at one and the same time, a new language. This might appear to be illogical. However, the logic of miracle inheres in precisely the fact that it surpasses logic. A miracle that rests on logic ceases to be a miracle.

THE SURAH'S QUR'ANIC PERSONA

As we have had to occasion to note, the Qur'an makes use of the verb normally translated as "was" (*kāna*) to mean "is." This new usage of the verb *kāna* recurs no fewer than 190 times in the Qur'an. Nevertheless, there has been no instance of this verb's being used in its new Qur'anic sense in any other piece of writing to this day. This applies even to the Prophetic hadith. However, the distribution of this use of the verb *kāna* across the various surahs of the Qur'an is even more remarkable. It is quite natural that a short, two-line surah such as *Sūrah al-Ikhlāṣ* (112) would contain only one of the 190 instances of this use of the verb *kāna.*[6] Yet, quite contrary to what we would expect, statistically speaking, we find that *Sūrah al-Baqarah* (2), which makes up nearly 1/12 of the entire Qur'an, lacks a single instance of this use of the verb *kāna* (meaning the use of *kāna* to mean "is" rather than "was").

So what of other surahs that are only slightly shorter, such as *Sūrah Āl ᶜImrān* (3), *Sūrah al-Mā'idah* (5), *Sūrah al-Anᶜām* (6), *Sūrah al-Aᶜrāf* (7), *Sūrah al-Anfāl* (8) and *Sūrah al-Tawbah* (9)? None of them contains a single instance. And thus the situation remains up to the sixteenth surah, *Sūrah al-Naḥl.* In fact, instances of this new and peculiar usage of the verb *kāna* are missing from surahs that make up nearly the first half of the Qur'an.

However, in the midst of this vast stretch of flatland there suddenly looms a towering peak, namely, *Sūrah al-Nisā'* (4), where, in a radical break with the prevailing pattern, the new use of the verb *kāna* recurs 53 times. It then disappears again until *Sūrah al-Isrā'* (17), where it is repeated a hefty 27 times. Then it disappears again for seven more surahs and reappears in *Sūrah al-Furqān* (25), where it is repeated 11 times, after which it disappears for seven more surahs until it appears in *Sūrah al-Aḥzāb* (33), where it recurs 26 times. It then appears successively in a number of the later surahs.

This phenomenon supports our contention that each surah in the Qur'an has its own impenetrable wall of sorts, and a distinct linguistic stamp that sets it apart from the others such that it would be difficult for the verses of one surah to mingle or overlap with those of another.

A still more important aspect of this phenomenon is that it serves to confirm the current place of each surah in relation to all others in the Qur'an while ruling out the occurrence of any sort of human modification of the ordering that has come down to us. In opposition to the unjustified and prejudiced claims made by certain Orientalists, this phenomenon argues in favor of those who assert that the order in which the surahs are presently arranged is of divine origin, while confirming that the surahs are arranged in the same sequence in which they were arranged in the days of the Prophet.

The linguistic stamp that marks each individual surah is a remarkable Qur'anic phenomenon which forms part of the structure and persona of the Qur'an as a whole. As will become clear from our detailed study of the surahs, each surah is set apart by the use of terms that are not found in any other surahs, and by new linguistic relationships, formulations, and constructions that mark that particular surah alone. There is, in addition, a distinctive overall rhythm and rhyme that permeate each individual surah and no other.

DO THE CHARACTERS OF THE SURAHS OVERLAP?

When memorizing some surahs, particularly the shorter ones, we may feel as though we are about to shift accidentally from reciting one surah to reciting another that shares in the same rhythm and that has certain rhyme letters in common with the one we are reciting. This may happen, for example, in relation to *Sūrah al-Mursalāt* (77) and *Sūrah al-Nāziᶜāt* (79), *Sūrah al-Takwīr* (81) and *Sūrah al-Inshiqāq* (84), or *Sūrah al-Aᶜlā* (87) and *Sūrah al-Layl* (92). This kind of accidental shifting from one surah to another might lead us to think that there is some overlap between the characters of the two surahs concerned, and that the boundaries between them are sufficiently blurred that one might melt into the other, in which case our claim that each surah has its own unique linguistic character would be shown to be unfounded.

Sūrah al-Aᶜlā (87) and Sūrah al-Layl (92)

However, a quick comparison between any two surahs, however similar they may appear to be, will show how different their linguistic characters actually are, and that they hardly have a single phrase in common. As an example, let us take *Sūrah al-Aᶜlā* (87) and *Sūrah al-Layl* (92) and examine their respective linguistic structures and expressions. This comparison will make clear how disparate these two surahs' linguistic personalities actually are despite their overlapping rhythmic lines.

Sūrah al-Aᶜlā consists of 72 words, while *Sūrah al-Layl* consists of 71 words. Yet despite the fact that the two surahs have a similar rhyme whereby each verse or *āyah* ends with an *alif*, the final word in the verse generally following the pattern *faᶜlā* (فَعْلَى), and despite the fact that they have a limited number of words in common (*khalaqa*, *al-ashqā*, *yaṣlā*, *al-ākhirah*, *rabbahu*, and *al-aᶜlā*), this is where the commonalities end. Apart from the aforementioned similarities, each of these two surahs has its own distinct and disparate expressions, idioms and structures. Still more peculiar, and more miraculous, is the fact that most of the structures and expressions of which each of the two surahs consists are unique to each of them respectively.

Of the 26 structures and expressions that make up the bulk of *Sūrah al-Aʿlā*, we find no more than four in other surahs of the Qur'an. These are *khalaqa fa sawwā*, *illā mā shā'a Allāh*, *fa dhakkir*, and *wa lā yaḥyā*, whereas 22 of them – or more than 80 percent of these structures and expressions – are unique to this surah alone and occur nowhere else.

As for *Sūrah al-Layl*, of the 25 structures and expressions that go to make it up, we only find three expressions which it shares with other surahs, namely, *fa andhartukum*, *kadhdhaba wa tawallā*, and *illā ibtighā'a*. However, the remaining 22 structures and expressions, or 88 percent of the total, are found in no other surah, including, of course, *Sūrah al-Aʿlā*.

THE QUR'AN'S UNIQUE CHARACTER

As soon as the process of revelation began, the Arabs who heard the Qur'an realized instinctively that everything relating to it suggested newness and singularity. These qualities could be perceived in its distinctive name, "Qur'an," which pre-Islamic Arabs had never used before, and the uniqueness of the book's title pointed to the uniqueness of its content. The same newness and singularity are reflected in the title given to the Qur'an's opening chapter, *al-Fātiḥah*, which was unique to the Qur'an alone. As for the word surah, which was used to refer to the Qur'an's sections or chapters, it was derived from the word *sūr* (سُور), which refers to a city wall or citadel. The meaning of this term was like a heavenly sign pointing to the impregnability of the Quran's "walls" and the impossibility of either imitating its chapters (surahs) or finding gaps or breaches that would allow someone to make his way inside them. Next we come to the term *āyah,* meaning sign or miracle, which God used to refer to the verses of the Qur'an.

In this designation we have another divine hint pointing to the miraculous character of the book as a whole and to the element of challenge inherent in every one of its linguistic units, be it long or short. And lastly we come to the term *tilāwah*. Derived from the verb *yatlū* (يتلو) meaning to follow or come after, the word *tilāwah* came to be applied to the recitation of the Qur'an in a reminder from Heaven that the Messenger of God was not the first person to have recited the Qur'an's verses on earth but was, rather, "a follower" in its recitation, since Gabriel had been the first to recite them, and the Prophet had "followed him" (*talāhu* تلاه) by imitating the angel's recitation, and we follow the Prophet.

It should be stressed here that the Holy Qur'an is the only book in the world which, to this day, has continued to be marked by features that it shares with no other book on Earth. The comparison being made here is not based on the books' subject matter, ideas, language, or style. After all, every book in the world is bound to have certain features that set it apart from all others in relation to its topic, the ideas it presents, and its linguistic style. Rather, what I am speaking of here is the "genus" of book qua book.

If, for example, you compared the book in your hands now with any other book in your library, you would find nothing that set it apart from the others insofar as it is a book. We might, of course, compare a book written in English with a book written in Arabic, in which case we could say that each of the two books is distinguished by two features: (1) the language in which it was written (one in English, the other in Arabic), and (2) the direction in which it is read (the one in English being read from left to right, and the one in Arabic being read from right to left). This is the extent of the difference between these two books. However, neither of these books is distinguished from all other books in the world by either of these features. There are millions of other books in the world that have been written in Arabic or in English. The Qur'an, by contrast, is marked by a number of features that it shares with no other book on the face of the Earth, and no other book in the history of humankind. I have counted up twenty such distinguishing features, twelve of which I list below:

1. Unique terms are used to refer to its chapters and verses.

2. It can be read in more than one way, with all these ways being viewed as divinely inspired.

3. The way it is recited differs from the way it is written. Examples of this include the words for prayer (*al-ṣalāh*), alms tax (*al-zakāh*) and life (*al-ḥayāh*), which are written in the Qur'an with the letter *wāw* (representing a long 'u' sound) although we read it as an *alif* (which represents an 'a' sound as in the word 'cat'). Another example is the word *qawārīrā* in *Sūrah al-Insān* 76:16, which is recited without the final extra *alif* "a" sound although it appears in the written word.

4. Its text is pronounced differently from any other Arabic text in the world. This differing manner of pronunciation has been elaborated in detail through the art of *tajwīd*, or Qur'anic recitation, in keeping with established rules of pronunciation and intonation.

5. It is written differently than any other Arabic text. (This is due to the fact that the spelling rules on the basis of which the Qur'an is written differ from those used in modern Arabic, as well as from those that were used fourteen centuries ago.)

6. It can only be documented based on having heard it recited aloud by others. In addition to reliance on the rules of *tajwīd*, documentation of the Qur'an depends on an oral chain of transmission that goes back to the Prophet Muhammad himself.

7. The Qur'an is recited melodically. As the Prophet commanded, "Recite the Qur'an with a melody, he will be not one of us who does not recite it in this manner,"[7] "not one of us" meaning that he is not following the way of the Prophet.

8. The linguistic style of the Qur'an is entirely different from that of the person who delivered it to us, that is, the Prophet Muhammad.

9. Millions of people throughout the world have memorized it from cover to cover.

10. Most of those who have memorized the Qur'an do not speak Arabic and do not even understand it. Arabs make up no more than 20 percent of the world's Muslims.

11. The various texts of the Qur'an are confirmed millions of times a day. It is recited aloud three times a day: at the dawn prayer (*al-fajr*), the sundown prayer (*al-maghrib*), and the final evening prayer (*al-ᶜishā'*) in the context of communal prayers all over the world. This is in addition to the communal Friday prayer and the communal prayers conducted on the occasions of ᶜ*Īd al-Fiṭr* and ᶜ*Īd al-Aḍḥā*. These prayers have taken place in hundreds of thousands of mosques the world over for fourteen centuries, ever since the command to pray was issued. If the prayer leader mispronounces a word or makes any other error in his recitation, he will be corrected immediately by scores of worshippers who are praying behind him. This remarkable, intensive method of authentication makes it impossible for so much as a single word or letter to be omitted from or added to the Qur'an, or for any word or phrase to be corrupted in any way.

12. The Qur'an ignited the most widespread scientific revolution the world has ever known, and in record time. Apart from the Qur'an, no single book in the history of humankind has ever brought about a literary, scientific, intellectual and linguistic revolution in the space of only a few decades, and on an isolated, unlettered peninsula among whose inhabitants the Bible was the only book in circulation.

THE NEW LINGUISTIC FORMULATION

Like the litterateurs of other language groups, the pre-Islamic poets developed a pool of commonly used linguistic structures from which they drew for expressing their ideas and from which they rarely departed. As a consequence, they came to have set molds or templates that provided the linguistic backdrop to their poetry. We can trace most extant pre-Islamic poetry back to several hundred basic linguistic templates that were in circulation in the poetic market prior to the appearance of the Qur'anic revelation, and which made up what might be termed the infrastructure of the pre-Islamic *qaṣīdah*, or poem. Many of these templates continued to be used after the revelation of the Qur'an, and some of them are still employed by many poets with varying degrees of frequency. These templates were on the order of primary linguistic units that served as the basis for the overall structure of a poem or literary text, and only rarely would a poet, writer, or orator deviate from them or introduce a new template to enrich the old linguistic structure.

These literary templates might be likened to pieces of a jigsaw puzzle or playing cards. Litterateurs would have ready-made pieces with which to form linguistic figures – their poems or literary pieces. Thus formed, poems might look new to the outside observer. In reality they were nothing but old molds or raw materials that had been used to create new forms. An overview of the opening lines of selected pre-Islamic poems is sufficient to illustrate the magnitude and frequency of this phenomenon in ancient Arabic poetry: *wa man yaku dhā, wa innī imru'un in…, alā hal atā* ^{c}*annā…, alā layta shi*^{c}*rī hal…., alā an*^{c}*im ṣabāhan ayyuhā al-rab*^{c}*…, khalīlayya murra bī…., amin āli asmā' al-ṭulūl al-dawārisu…, yā ṣāḥibayya talawamā, waddi*^{c} *umāmata inna…, ahājaka min asmā'a rasmu al-manāzili…, samā laka shawqun ba*^{c}*da mā kāna…, liman ṭalalun bayna al-jadiyah….*

As for the language of the Qur'anic revelation, it turned everything upside down. It shattered the old, inherited molds and rent the traditional linguistic fabric to weave a fabric of its own and to cast new linguistic molds that were destined to send tremors through the length and breadth of the Arabs' literary language. These new forms were not limited to one part or aspect of the Qur'an. Rather, they encompassed the book in its entirety, with the result that once people had become familiar with its language, they could easily recognize the "Qur'anness" of even a random sample consisting of nothing but a single phrase, expression or construction drawn from any part of the book.

MOST QUR'ANIC LINGUISTIC FORMS DO NOT REPEAT THEMSELVES

The unique "flavor" of Qur'anic linguistic constructions might lead us to believe that they are repeated many times throughout the holy book so that, despite their newness and their distinctness from the constructions that are well known in the Arabic language used both today and in the days of the Prophet, it is this repetition that enables us to recognize them easily as being Qur'anic in nature. Surprisingly, however, and despite the fact that there clearly is repetition in the Qur'an, the Qur'anic constructions which are *not* repeated are far greater in number than those which are. In fact, most of the uniquely Qur'anic constructions and expressions occur only once, and no more. Yet in spite of this fact, they retain their clear, distinctive flavor. As for the constructions used in non-Qur'anic Arabic, whether in poetry or in prose, we find it difficult to recognize them and retain their forms and structures unless they are repeated enough times for us to grow accustomed to seeing and hearing them. Hence, another remarkable feature of the language of the Holy Qur'an is the ease with which we become familiar with its forms and structures even when they are not repeated.

Someone might object here, saying: Why claim that the Qur'an alone contains unique turns of phrase? After all, every writer on earth has his or her unique manner of expression and turns of phrase that are peculiar to his or her writing. This is true, of course, to some extent. However, no matter how much human linguistic styles may differ from one another and no matter how far apart they may be in terms of time and place, they do not always enable us to distinguish their authors one from another. It is not uncommon for two or more writers to have such similar styles that we get them confused. This fact will be clear to us if we take a single sentence from one writer's corpus and compare it with sentences produced by other writers. We might, for example, make a random selection of statements made by five Arab writers from various literary periods – al-Maʿarrī, Ibn al-Muqaffaʿ, Ibn Ḥazm, Taha Husayn, and Mustafa Sadiq al-Rafii – and ask someone to match the statements with their authors. The statements are as follows:

1. *Wa ammā al-kitābu fa jamaʿa ḥikmatan wa lahwan*

   وأمّا الكتابُ فجمَعَ حكمةً ولهواً

2. *Wa inna hādha la yuwallidu min al-ḥuzni wa al-asafi ghayra qalīlin*

   وإنّ هذا لَيولّدُ من الحُزنِ والأسفِ غيرَ قَلِيلٍ

3. *Yabtadiʿūn asālība wa manāhija fī naẓmi al-kalām*

   يبتدعون أساليبَ ومناهجَ في نظم الكلام

4. *Lā yakhāfu ʿalā waladihi min al-yutm*

   لا يخافُ على ولدِه من اليُتم

5. *Wa lākinna al-fanna al-bayāniyya yartafiʿu ʿalā dhālika*

   ولكنّ الفنّ البيانيّ يرتفعُ على ذلك

No matter how literarily skilled and sophisticated he or she happened to be and no matter how insightful a critic, even a native speaker of

Arabic would find it impossible to match these passages correctly with their authors unless it should happen by chance.[8] If, on the other hand, we introduced a verse from the Qur'an – any verse, be it long or short – along with these five statements by human authors, taken though they are from entirely different periods and originating from disparate literary schools, it would be easy for the most unpracticed reader of the Qur'an to distinguish it as having come from the Holy Book.

INTENSIVE UNIQUE QUR'ANIC CONSTRUCTIONS

There is an abundance of uniquely Qur'anic constructions and expressions that do not repeat themselves, and we can easily identify a good number of them on any single page of the Qur'an. In order to ensure that our conclusions are objective and comprehensive rather than subjective and selective, we might take the first complete page of the Qur'anic text which, in most printed copies, contains verses 6–16 of *Sūrah al-Baqarah*. Even this small sample will make clear how numerous and varied such constructions and expressions are. On this one page alone we find at least 23 of them, and each of them has a singular structure that sets it apart, not only from expressions and constructions found widely in Arabic poetry and prose and those that occur in the Prophetic traditions but, in addition, from the other expressions and constructions on the very same page of the Qur'an itself. We will see that, in addition to their uniqueness and distinctness, and despite the Qur'an's influence on the Arabic language as a whole and the attraction its refined style has held for Arab writers down the ages, most of these expressions and constructions have remained unique to the Qur'an itself and hence easily distinguishable from human linguistic expression. Nor will we find a similar phenomenon in any other literary language down the ages. The following are the structures to which I am referring in the passage selected:

1. **Verse 6**: *sawā'un ʿalayhim a'andhartahum am lam tundhirhum, la yu'minūn* ("it is all one to them whether thou warnest them or dost not warn them: they will not believe").

2. **Verse 7:** *wa lahum ʿadhābun ʿaẓīm* ("and awesome suffering awaits them").

3. **Verse 8a:** *wa mina al-nāsi man yaqūlu āmannā* ("And there are people who say, 'We do believe...'").

4. **Verse 8b:** *wa mā hum bi mu'minīn* ("the while they do not [really] believe").

5. **Verse 9:** *wa mā yakhdaʿūna illā anfusahum ma mā yashʿurūn* ("the while they deceive none but themselves, and perceive it not").

6. **Verse 10a:** *fī qulūbihim maraḍun fa zādahum Allāhu maraḍan* ("In their hearts is disease, and so God lets their disease increase").

7. **Verse 10b:** *wa lahum ʿadhābun alīm* ("and grievous suffering awaits them"). Here we have a repetition of Construction 2 above.

8. **Verse 10c:** *bi mā kānū yakdhibūn* ("because of their persistent lying").

9. **Verse 11a:** *wa idhā qīla lahum lā tufsidū fī al-arḍ* ("And when they are told, 'Do not spread corruption on earth,'...").

10. **Verse 11b:** *qālū innamā naḥnu muṣliḥūn* ("they say, 'We are but improving things!'").

11. **Verse 12a:** *alā innahum hum al-mufsidūn* ("Oh, verily, it is they, they who are spreading corruption").

12. **Verse 12b:** *wa lākin lā yashʿurūn* ("but they perceive it not").

13. **Verse 13a:** *wa idhā qīla lahum āminū kamā āman al-nāsu* ("And when they are told, 'Believe as other people believe,'....").

14. **Verse 13b:** *qālū anu'minu kamā āmana al-sufahā'u*
("they answer, 'Shall we believe as the weak-minded believe?'...").

15. **Verse 13c:** *alā innahum hum al-sufahā'u*
("Oh, verily, it is they, they who are weak-minded"). This is a repetition of Construction 11 above.

16. **Verse 13d:** *wa lākin lā yaʿlamūn* ("but they know it not").
A repetition of Construction 12 above.

17. **Verse 14a:** *wa idhā laqu alladhīna āmanū qālū āmannā*
("And when they meet those who have attained to faith, they assert...").

18. **Verse 14b:** *wa idhā khalaw ilā shayāṭīnihim*
("But when they find themselves alone with their evil impulses...").

19. **Verse 14c:** *qālū innamā naḥnu mustahzi'ūn*
("they say, 'Verily, we are with you. We were only mocking'"). A repetition of Construction 10 above.

20. **Verse 15a:** *Allāhu yastahzi'u bihim*
("God will requite them for their mockery [or: God will mock at them]").

21. **Verse 15b:** *wa yamudduhum fī ṭughyānihim yaʿmahūn*
("and will leave them for a while in their overweening arrogance, blindly stumbling to and fro").

22. **Verse 16a:** *ulā'ika alladhīna ishtaraw al-ḍalālata bil-hudā*
("[for] it is they who have taken error in exchange for guidance").

23. **Verse 16b:** *wa mā kānū muhtadīn*
("...nor have they found guidance").

As can be seen from the listing above, four of the Qur'anic constructions in this passage are repeated twice. However, none of the 23 constructions and expressions listed here resembles any construction or expression found in non-Qur'anic Arabic, including that used in the Prophetic hadiths. Hence, if we were to mingle any of these expressions or constructions with those employed in Arabic poetry or prose, readers could easily pick them out as being from the Qur'an and from nowhere else.

How, then, did the Arabs living on the Arabian Peninsula in the seventh century CE cope with this expressional storm that blew over them from Makkah? Where did the language of the Holy Qur'an stand in relation to the massive linguistic tradition that had flowered in the pre-Islamic era? What reaction would be forthcoming from the Arabs who, up to that time, had been accustomed to trading in a linguistic market that offered no more than a few hundred basic recurring linguistic templates or patterns when, all of a sudden, they came in contact with a book packed with thousands of new linguistic forms that had been unknown to their poetry and prose alike, and that would remain unknown to Arabic literary production thereafter?

QUR'ANIC LINGUISTIC TEMPLATES: THEIR NATURE AND COMPOSITION

The singularity that manifests itself on the level of the Qur'an's patterns and individual words, as well as in relations among words, constructions, and expressions, serves to create a distinctive language that even the ordinary reader would find it difficult to confuse with recognized human styles. What enables us to tell the difference between a Qur'anic statement and a merely human statement is not the distinctive Qur'anic terms alone. It is not the constructions on which the Qur'anic language is built or their lilting cadence. It is not the new Qur'anic images that so astonish us, nor the divinely inspired messages with their wisdom, solemnity, gravity and timelessness and the ability to soar above and beyond merely human messages and qualities. Nor is it the distinct heavenly discourse which is so fully capable, confident, masterful, knowledgeable, authoritative, and exalted above the weak human spirit. The distinctive quality of the Qur'anic text goes beyond all of this to the way in which all these elements are cast together into linguistic units and patterns which, even if they were mingled with thousands of human statements, clauses, phrases and the like, they would declare themselves unmistakably as being Qur'anic in origin.

The slightest change in a Qur'anic pattern or template will cause it to lose its meter. And in fact, there are as many meters as there are Qur'anic linguistic patterns. These meters are not based on vowels and non-vowelled consonants as they are in regular prosody. Nor are they based on the human rules that govern the arrangement and homogeneity of letters. In fact, the Qur'anic patterns of which we speak deviate from these rules on innumerable occasions, yet this very deviation renders them all the more fluid and masterful. The following verse, for example, contains six *mīms* in close succession: *wa man aẓlamu mimman manaʿa masājida Allāhi an yudhkara fīhā ismuhu* ("Hence, who could be more wicked than those who bar the mention of [God's] name from [any of] His houses of worship...." – *Sūrah al-Baqarah* 2:114). When read according to the rules of *tajwīd*,[9] they come out as: *wa man aẓlamu mimmamma* – ومَن أظلمُ مِمْ مَمْ مَـ .... In *Sūrah Hūd* 11:48 we have eight *mīms* in close succession: *wa ʿalā umamin mimman maʿaka* ("...upon thee, as well as upon the people [who are with thee...]"), and which, when read according to the rules of *tajwīd*, are pronounced, *umamim mimmam ma*...وعلى أمَمِمْ مِمْمَمْ مَعك. Yet, in spite of this long succession of *mīms*, they are not felt to be heavy or cumbersome the way they would if we encountered them in some text of human origin.

The meter, or Qur'anic rhythm, emerges from other subtle factors and elements which our existing critical tools are, in my opinion, still unable to help us pinpoint and define. This observation has been confirmed by a number of Western thinkers who have developed a feel for the Qur'an through their study of it, and who have described the peculiar psychological impact it had on them even though they did not understand what the text meant. Author Jeffrey Lang writes about such thinkers, saying:

> As many converts know, one does not have to be a Muslim to feel this intrinsic power of the Qur'an, for many of them chose Islam after, and because of, such moments. Also, many a non-Muslim scholar of the Qur'an has reported it. The British scholar of Arabic, Arthur J. Arberry, recalled how the Qur'an supported him through a difficult time in his life. He stated that listening to the Qur'an chanted in Arabic was, for him, like listening to the beat of his own heart. Fredrick Denny, a non-Muslim writer, recalls the "wonderfully disturbing experience" one sometimes has when reading the Qur'an, when the reader starts feeling "an uncanny, sometimes frightening presence." Instead of reading the Qur'an, the reader begins feeling the Qur'an is "reading" the reader![10]

However, in our preoccupation with describing the nature of the new Qur'anic linguistic fabric, we should not lose sight of the fact that this new fabric, in fact, has remained "new" to this very day. Everything a human being writes or says for the first time today is, with the passage of time, bound to become old. The linguistic patterns that were introduced by the first pre-Islamic poet were new when he first produced them. However, it wasn't long before they had become old hat, so to speak, something that was repeated over and over by one poet after another. As for the Qur'anic linguistic patterns, most of them brought time to a standstill at the moment when they were first revealed, since no number of repetitions could rob them of their newness.

The language used by the Prophet Muhammad took two distinctly different forms: *ḥadīth qudsī* (sacred narration) that is, sayings whose meaning the Prophet received by divine inspiration and which he conveyed in his own words; and normal hadith, sayings uttered by the Prophet himself using his own meanings and his own words. The language of the hadiths in both these forms was marked by an extraordinary degree of eloquence and beauty. At the same time, however, it retained certain human qualities that set it clearly and unambiguously apart from the inimitability of the divine speech found in the Qur'an. Imagine that a factory director gathers his employees together and gives them a speech in the course of which he wants to tell them that each of them is responsible for his own mistakes. In communicating this idea, he wants to draw on the well-known Qur'anic phrase, *wa lā taziru wizāratun wizra ukhrā* ("and no bearer of burdens shall be made to bear another's burden" *Sūrah Fāṭir* 35:18), but without quoting it directly. Hence, in an attempt to paraphrase it by replacing some of the Qur'anic terms with words of his own while keeping its linguistic structure as it is, he replaces the Arabic root *w – z – r* employed in this verse with words derived from the root *ḥ–m –l*, saying, *wa lā taḥmilu ḥāmilatun ḥimla ukhrā*. In borrowing this highly distinctive Qur'anic linguistic pattern, he goes beyond the act of quoting or paraphrasing. He keeps the structure unchanged while embedding words of his own, replacing the words used by the Qur'an with words bearing similar meanings and retaining the same meter. However, he ends up with nothing but a laughable linguistic contortion.

"PRODUCE THEN A SURAH LIKE UNTO IT" (Qur'an 10:38)

This is why our forefathers in the faith scoffed at people who made naïve attempts to detract from the Qur'an and from Islam by coming up with lame, garbled linguistic structures and claiming that they were surahs from the Qur'an. And it is why we laugh today when people keep on making such silly attempts. Try as they might to introduce into the Qur'an what is foreign to it or to formulate a sentence or even a phrase that rises to the level of the Qur'an's linguistic mastery, their forgery is exposed by the Qur'an's pristine singularity on the level of individual words and structures alike, just as DNA tests expose those who try to attribute a child to some man other than his or her actual father, or to hold someone responsible for an action he did not commit. The language of the Qur'an is bound to reject any new linguistic blood with which we might attempt to inject it, and in the course of its invasion, the incompatible blood group will corrupt whatever tissues it comes in contact with.

The Patterns that Marked the Speech of the Prophet

We have innumerable accounts of things said by the Messenger of God. So we might ask: Do the things that apply to the language of Heaven apply to his speech as well? Will we end up with nothing but a laughable, pathetic hodgepodge of words if we conduct the same experiment with the Prophet's words that we did above with a phrase from the Qur'an? How can we be certain that the language of the Prophet, however lofty, superior and singular its style happens to be, is also human speech that is subject to infiltration or forgery? Once again, in order to avoid falling into subjectivity and selectivity and in keeping with the principle of "take whatever comes" that we adopted in our study of the patterns found on the first page of the Qur'an and in our decision to focus our study on one of the earliest surahs (*Sūrah al-Muddaththir*), let us use a hadith that appears in the opening section of Imam al-Nawawī's *Riyāḍ al-Ṣāliḥīn* (Gardens of the Righteous), one of the most famed collections of Prophetic hadiths. In this hadith we encounter an unmistakable difference between God's speech and that of the Prophet:

> ʿUmar ibn al-Khaṭṭāb (may God be pleased with him), said, "I heard the Messenger of God (pbuh) say, 'The [essence of] an action lies in its [underlying] intention, and each individual [will be judged based on] whatever he or she intends. If someone migrates in order to be with God and His Messenger, he will be rewarded based on this intention. But if someone migrates for the sake of some worldly aim he hopes to fulfill or a woman he hopes to marry, he will be judged in accordance with this intention.'" (Agreed upon)[11]

Any one of us could easily construct an expression of his own based on the structure evident in the Prophet's opening words, *innamā al-aʿmālu bil-niyyāt* (translated above as, "The [essence of] an action lies in its [underlying] intention"). One might say for example, *innamā al-ʿibrah bil-natāʾij* ("The proof's in the pudding") without violating recognized linguistic conventions or finding himself the butt of ridicule or objections. It would be equally easy for you to base a statement of your own on the second linguistic pattern found in the aforementioned hadith, *wa innamā li kulli imri'in mā nawā* (translated as, "and each individual [will be judged based on] whatever he or she intends"). You might say, for example, *wa innamā li kulli mutasābiqin mā aḥraza* ("Every contestant is entitled to what he/she has earned") without feeling that the statement is awkward in any way or worrying that someone will respond to it with a sarcastic comment. Similarly, you might easily use ordinary language to form a statement based on the patterns found in the remainder of the hadith above. Emulating the pattern, *fa man kānat hijratuhu ilā Allāhi wa rasūlihi, fa hijratuhu ilā Allāhi wa rasūlihi* (translated as, "If someone migrates in order to be with God and His Messenger, he will be rewarded based on this intention"), you might say, *fa man kānat ghāyatuhu al-khayr, fa ajruhū ʿaẓīm* ("If someone's aim is to perform a good deed, his reward will be great"), and on the pattern of *wa man kānat hijratuhu li dunyā yuṣībuhā aw imra'atin yankiḥuha, fa hijratuhu ilā mā hājara ilayhi* (translated above as, "But if someone migrates for the sake of some worldly aim he hopes to fulfill or a woman he hopes to marry, he will be judged in accordance with this intention"), you might say, *wa man kānat ghāyatuhu mālan yarbaḥuhu aw shuhratan yanāluhā, fa ajruhu huwa mā ikhtāra li nafsihi* ("If someone's aim [in migrating] is to make money or achieve fame, then his or her reward will consist in whatever he has chosen for himself") without inviting ridicule or alienating those who read what you have written or hear what you have said.

The fact is that the corpus of genuine Prophetic hadiths has been infiltrated by thousands of forgeries. However, our scholars have managed to identify these alien, plagiarized hadiths. By virtue of their highly developed documentational methods, these scholars have been able to distinguish, with nearly perfect certainty, between authentic hadiths and forgeries. In a number of sayings that have come down to us, the Prophet Muhammad warned of the possibility of such infiltration, and he laid down more than one principle by means of which Muslims could distinguish his actual sayings from those interpolated by plagiarists with personal agendas to promote. In one such hadith, he states:

> If you hear a saying attributed to me which your hearts (minds) recognize, and if you feel that it is close to you, I will stand more ready to recognize it than you yourselves are. If, on the other hand, you hear a saying that has been attributed to me but your hearts recoil from it and you perceive it as being distant from you, I myself will be more distant from it than you are.[12]

We should also bear in mind that if we have three versions of a single authentic hadith, at least two of these versions are bound to contain some wording which differs from that used by the Prophet himself and which was suggested or imagined by the narrators who passed the tradition down. However, these slight alterations in wording do nothing to detract from or disrupt the Prophet's linguistic style.

NEWNESS OF CONSTRUCTION AND EXPRESSION

It goes without saying that when we study the constructions (*tarākīb*, singular, *tarkīb*), expressions (*taʿbīrāt*, singular, *taʿbīr*), patterns (*sabāʾik*, singular, *sabīkah*) and linguistic connections in the Qur'an, we may find it difficult at times to draw the lines clearly among these various elements. However, in this particular subsection we will attempt to remain within the linguistic region shared by what I am terming constructions (*tarākīb*) and expressions (*taʿbīrāt*). We will not, for example, venture into the realm of single words. Nor will we be dealing with linguistic units consisting of four words or more, since to do so would bring us into the region of the *sabīkah*, or pattern, which is a larger linguistic unit that may contain constructions and expressions, but which is not contained within a structure or expression. In the following discussion we will restrict ourselves to two- word or three-word formulations that manifest a new grammatical or rhetorical relationship that was not found in the Arabic language prior to the appearance of the Qur'an. The boundaries between constructions (*tarākīb*) and expressions (*ta*ʿ*bīrāt*) frequently overlap, which makes it difficult to distinguish between them at times. Hence, I have chosen for the purposes of this study to define the construction, or *tarkīb*, as a verbal formulation that does not communicate a complete idea and which consists primarily of particles, conjunctions, prepositions, single letters, and the like, while the expression, or *ta*ʿ*bīr*, is defined as a verbal formulation which communicates a complete, or nearly complete, idea, and which consists primarily of nouns or verbs.

The Qur'anic Construction (Tarkīb)

All at once, and within the short span of time it took for its revelation to be completed, the Qur'an brought the Arabs thousands of new constructions and expressions. These constructions and expressions fill the surahs of the Qur'an, both short and long, and many of them entered the Arabic language on the level of both literary production and daily usage, although most of them remained restricted to the Qur'an alone, as their intense distinctiveness precluded their infiltration of these other linguistic realms.

We may encounter scores of these constructions in every reading of the Qur'an. However, we do not stop to notice them, nor do we see anything unusual or perplexing about them. The reason for this is that we are so accustomed to the Qur'an that such phenomena are all we expect to find there. But if we took a good, long look at them, and if we emptied our memories of our familiarity with the language of the Qur'an and went back to our ordinary, everyday language, whether written or spoken, as though we had never known anything else, we would suddenly find ourselves face to face with an entirely new language that bears no connection to our everyday human language despite the fact that it is based on the same rules.

Qur'anic construction	Construction used in everyday Arabic	English translation
man dhā alladhī	*man alladhī*	Who is it that...?
hal ʿaṣaytum	*hal yuntaẓaru minkum*	Might you...?
fa'idh lam ya'tū	*fa mā dāmū ʿājizīn ʿan an ya'tū*	If they are unable to bring....
baʿda idh	*baʿda an*	After...
wa kadhālika jaʿalnā	*wa hākadhā jaʿalnā*	Thus We made...
wa'inna kullan lammā	*wa kullu wāḥidin minhum*	Every one of them...
in kāda la yuḍillunā	*kāda an yuḍillanā*	He nearly misled us...
awa law ji'tuka	*ḥatta in ji'tuka*	Even if I bring to you...
fa lammā an jā'a	*fa lammā jā'a*	When he came...
innā la naḥnu al-ghālibūn	*innanā sa naghlibuhum*	We will defeat them....
fīmā hāhunā āminīn	*āminīn hunā*	[You are] safe here...
qalilān mā	*mā aqalla*	Rarely...

Table 1: Comparison of new constructions in the Qur'an with everyday Arabic

A quick look at the above list of constructions, most of which occur repeatedly in the Qur'an, will be sufficient to show how different they are from the constructions Arabs use in their day-to-day lives.

Despite the rarity with which such constructions occur in general given the fact that, as we have noted, they consist primarily of particles, conjunctions, prepositions, single letters, and so on, we can locate the following (*see table 2*) twelve new constructions in *Sūrah al-Muddaththir*.

When we come to the question of how many new expressions are found in this surah, we might better ask whether this surah contains any expression that is *not* new. *Sūrah al-Muddaththir* consists of 56 verses which take up less than two pages. Nevertheless, we can count no fewer than 65 new Qur'anic expressions in this surah alone together with 12 new constructions, all of which occur in the space of

Construction	English translation	Verse
fa dhālika yawma'idhin	"that very day shall be .."	9
kallā innahu	"Nay, verily, it is…"	16
fa qutila kayfa	"and may death seize him for the way he…"[13]	19
thumma qutila kayfa	"Yea, may death seize him for the way he…."	20
in hādha illā	"All this is mere…"	24
wa mā adrāka mā	"And what could make thee conceive what…?"	27
ka dhālika yuḍillu	"Thus doth God leave to stray…."	31
kallā wa al-qamari	"Nay, verily, by the moon!"	32
lam naku min	"We were not among…"	43
fa mā lahum ʿan	"What, then is amiss with them…"	49
kallā bal lā	"Nay, but they…not…"	53
illā an yashā' [Allāh]	"unless [God] so wills…"	56

Table 2: Twelve new constructions in *Sūrah al-Muddaththir*

a mere 56 verses, at least 30 of which consist of only two or three words. What this means is that this surah hardly contains any expressions that were already familiar to Arabs prior to the descent of the Qur'an. Even more extraordinary and exciting is the fact that 52 of these 65 new expressions occur nowhere but in this particular surah. This confirms once again, not only the newness of the Qur'an's language but, in addition, the fact that every surah of the Qur'an is marked by its own distinctive linguistic personality. This is a phenomenon that we will encounter repeatedly in our study of the short surahs in Volume Two.

Table 3 below depicts the 65 new expressions found in *Sūrah al-Muddaththir.*

No.	Expression	English translation	Verse
1	*yā ayyuhā al-muddaththir*	"O thou [in thy solitude] enfolded"	1
2	*qum fa andhir*	"Arise and warn!"	2
3	*wa rabbaka fa kabbir*	"And thy Sustainer's greatness glorify!"	3
4	*wa thiyābaka fa ṭahhir*	"And thine inner self [or, thy garments] purify!"	4
5	*wa al-rujza fahjur*	"And all defilement shun!"	5
6	*wa lā tamnun tastakthir*	"And do not through giving seek thyself to gain"	6
7	*wa li rabbika faṣbir*	"and unto thy Sustainer turn in patience."	7
8	*fa idhā nuqira fī al-nāqūr*	"And [warn all men that] when the trumpet call [of resurrection] is sounded"	8
9	*yawmun ʿasīr*	"…a day of anguish"	9
10	*ʿalā al-kāfirīna ghayru yasīr*	"not of ease, for all who [now] deny the truth!"	10
11	*dharnī wa man khalaqtu waḥīdan*	"Leave me alone [to deal] with him whom I have created alone"	11
12	*wa jaʿaltu lahu mālan*	"and to whom I have granted resources…"	12
13	*mālan mamdūdan*	"resources vast"	12
14	*banīna shuhūdan*	"and children as [love's] witnesses"	13
15	*mahhadtu lahu tamhīdan*	"to whose life I gave so wide a scope"	14
16	*yaṭmaʿu an azīd*	"he greedily desires that I give yet more!"	15
17	*kāna li āyātinā ʿanīdan*	"it is against Our messages that he knowingly, stubbornly sets himself"	16
18	*sa urhiquhu ṣaʿūdan*	"I shall constrain him to endure a painful uphill climb!"	17
19	*fakkara waqaddara*	"For he thought and he plotted"	18

No.	Expression	English translation	Verse
20	*fa qutila kayfa qaddar*	"and may death seize him for the way he meditates..."	19
21	*ʿabasa wa basar*	"then he frowned and stared"	22
22	*adbara wa istakbar*	"he turns his back [on Our message], and glories in his arrogance"	23
23	*siḥrun yu'thar*	"spellbinding eloquence handed down [from olden times]!"	24
24	*sa'uṣlīhi saqar*	"I shall cause him to endure hell-fire"	26
25	*lā tubqī wa lā tadhar*	"It does not allow to live, and neither leaves [to die]"	28
26	*lawwāḥatun lil-bashar*	"making [all truth] visible to mortal man"	29
27	*aṣḥāba al-nār*	"to lord over the fire [of hell]"	31
28	*wa mā jaʿalnā ʿiddatahum*	"We have not caused their number"	31
29	*fitnatan lil-ladhīna kafarū*	"a trial for those who are bent on denying the truth"	31
30	*alladhīna ūtū al-kitāb*	"they who have been granted revelation aforetime"	31
31	*yazdāda alladhīna āmanū īmānan*	"that they who have attained to faith [in it] might grow yet more firm in their faith"	31
32	*fī qulūbihim maraḍun*	"they in whose hearts is disease"	31
33	*[mādha] arāda Allāhu bi hādha mathalan*	"[What] does [your] God mean by this parable?"	31
34	*yuḍillu Allāhu man yashā'*	"Thus doth God leave to stray"	31
35	*wa yahdī man yashā'*	"and guide whom He pleaseth"	31

No.	Expression	English translation	Verse
36	*junūda rabbika*	"thy Sustainer's forces"	31
37	*dhikrā lil-bashar*	"a reminder to mortal man"	31
38	*kallā wa al-qamar*	"Nay, verily by the moon!"	32
39	*wa al-layli idh adbar*	"the night when it departs"	33
40	*wa al-ṣubḥi idha asfar*	"and the morn when it dawns"	34
41	*la iḥdā al-kubar*	"one of the great [forewarnings]"	35
42	*nadhīran lil-bashar*	"a warning to mortal man"	36
43	*an yataqaddama aw yata'akhkhar*	"to come forward or to hang back"	37
44	*bi mā kasabat rahīnah*	"will be held in pledge for whatever [evil] he has wrought"	38
45	*aṣḥāb al-yamīn*	"those who shall have attained to righteousness"	39
46	*fī jannātin yatasā'alūn*	"[dwelling] in gardens [of paradise], they will inquire"	40
47	*yatasā'alūna ᶜan al-mujrimīn*	"they will inquire of those who were lost in sin"	40–41
48	*mā salakakum fī saqar*	"What has brought you into hell-fire?"	42
49	*lam naku min al-muṣallīn*	"We were not among those who prayed"	43
50	*wa lam naku nuṭᶜim al-miskīn*	"and neither did we feed the needy"	44
51	*nakhūḍu maᶜa al-khā'iḍīn*	"we were wont to indulge in sinning together with all [the others] who indulged in it"	45
52	*yawm al-dīn*	"the Day of Judgment"	46
53	*nukadhdhibu bi yawm al-dīn*	"and the Day of Judgment we were wont to call a lie"	46
54	*atānā al-yaqīn*	"until certainty came upon us [in death]"	47

No.	Expression	English translation	Verse
55	*shafāʿat al-shāfiʿīn*	"the intercession of any that would intercede for them"	48
56	*ʿan al-tadhkirati muʿriḍīn*	"they turn away from all admonition"	49
57	*ḥumurun mustanfirah*	"terrified asses"	50
58	*farrat min qaswarah*	"fleeing from a lion"	51
59	*yu'tā ṣuḥufan munashsharah*	"to have been given revelations unfolded"	52
60	*lā yakhāfūn al-ākhirah*	"they do not fear the life to come"	53
61	*innahu tadhkirah*	"this is an admonition"	54
62	*fa man shā'a dhakarah*	"whoever wills may take it to heart"	55
63	*yashā' Allāh*	"God so wills"	56
64	*ahlu al-taqwā*	"the Fount of all God-consciousness"	56
65	*ahlu al-maghfirah*	"the Fount of all forgiveness"	56

Table 3: Depicting the 65 new expressions found in *Sūrah al-Muddaththir*

With the exception of the two expressions, *lā tubqī wa lā tadhar* in verse 28, and *yashā' Allāh* in verse 56, both of which later came to be used in both formal and, to a lesser extent, informal non-Qur'anic Arabic, the remaining expressions have remained restricted to the Qur'an alone.

INDIVIDUAL WORDS AND THE MIRACLE OF COMBINING NEWNESS AND CLARITY

The Qur'an is replete with new words, a fact that has prompted numerous Western skeptics to claim that the language of the Qur'an is not true Arabic. Such skeptics seem not to have noticed that the Qur'an itself states explicitly, and in more than one place, that it was revealed "in the clear Arabic tongue" (*Sūrah al-Shuʿarā'* 26:195).

A recent proponent of an extreme form of this view is German Orientalist, Christoph Luxenberg, who in his book, *The Syro-Aramaic Reading of the Koran*, published in Germany in 2000, claims that that Qur'an was "forged" by Muhammad, who derived it from Christian texts. The notion that the Qur'an is derived from Christian sources is harped on continuously by Orientalists and Christian evangelists alike. According to Luxenburg, the language of the Qur'an is not Arabic, but, rather, what he terms Syro-Aramaic, the language spoken by the merchants who once frequented Makkah and mixed with its inhabitants. Luxenberg goes so far as to say that in light of this "fact," the meanings of the Qur'an turn out to be entirely different from what Muslim interpreters have thought them to be.[14]

Needless to say Luxenberg's thesis of the Qur'an having Syro-Aramaic origins has been widely discredited by scholars, both Muslim and non-Muslim, despite the hype and fanfare which often accompanies such demonstrably false accusations.

In actual fact, contrary to the claim being made by Luxenberg, the new words contained in the Qur'an occur in forms that adhere to criteria that lie at the heart of the Arabic language and its linguistic rules. Hardly a single term in the entire Qur'an departs from these forms. Moreover, the new words introduced by the Qur'an occur in unique linguistic contexts that enable readers to realize what they mean despite their newness. Hence, the combination of newness and clarity is still another aspect of the innovative miracle manifested in the language of the Qur'an.

THE IMPORTANCE OF THE NEW TERMS FOUND IN THE QUR'AN

It was considered a major event for an Arab poet or litterateur to introduce a new term, especially if the term concerned had such a powerful impact on people's hearts and minds that it entered people's day-to-day conversation and was taken up and used by other writers and poets. The appearance of such a word even once in a given poet's production might even lead others to refer to the poet by this word until it replaced his original name. We find, for example, that the pre-Islamic poet al-Nābighah al-Dhubyānī (d. 604 CE) acquired the name by which he came to be known through his saying, *fa qad* ***nabaghat*** *lanā minhum shu'ūnun*, فقد نبغَتْ لنا منهم شؤونٌ; al-Muraqqash al-Akbar received this name based on his saying, ***raqqasha*** *fī ẓahr al-adīmi qalam*, رقَّش في ظهرِ الأديم قلم , while the title accorded to al-Musayyab ibn ʿAlas (d. 575 CE) originated in his saying, *ghizāran fa qūlū* ***lil-musayyabi*** *yalḥaqi*, غِزاراً فقولوا للمسيَّبِ يَلْحق .

When we study the language of the Holy Qur'an, there are certain facts we need to keep in mind in connection with its new terms in particular. It would be easy even for a young child to invent any number of new words once he has twenty-nine letters at his disposal. He can rearrange these letters however he likes to form literally millions of new words. But the important questions are: Who will understand these words later on, and what is their literary value? It is here that the reality of the Qur'anic miracle manifests itself most clearly. For not only did the desert Arabs of the seventh century understand the new text that was being presented to them from the first moment they heard it despite the fact that it brought them a language that was new in all of its fundamental elements and dimensions: its words, its particles, nouns and verbs, its constructions, expressions and patterns, the relationships among its words, its new grammatical conventions, its new concepts and legal rulings, its historical reports, and its scientific facts. Their response went beyond that of merely understanding what they were hearing to feeling an admiration so intense that it bordered on stupefaction, and the spontaneous acknowledgment of believers and skeptics alike of its superiority and the impossibility of attaining its heights.

The new Qur'anic terms can easily be classified into one of the following five groups:

1. Words that were already known to the Arabs, but which the Qur'an invested with new meanings that could be understood based on the linguistic or rhetorical context in which they occurred. Examples of such words include: *sulṭān* (authority), *maraḍ* (disease, a metaphor for unfaithfulness), *tawallā* (turn away), *aslama* (surrender oneself [to God]), *al-dunyā* (the earthly realm, earthly life), *al-ṣāliḥāt* (righteous actions), *al-shuhadā'* (martyrs), *al-rūḥ* (spirit, soul, the angel Gabriel), *khāshiʿīn* (reverent), *nabtahilu* (bringing supplication before God), *iṣr* (burden, a metaphor for the forbidden), *kitāb* (a divine revelation), *al-bayyinah* (evidence, a metaphor for the Islamic revelation), *al-birr* (piety, righteousness), *ʿiwaj* (crookedness), *al-ḥarth* (crops, tilling, tilth, a metaphor for a man's wife), *yanẓurūn* (consider, judge), *yasṭūn* (assault, attack), *al-muhtadūn* (guided aright, a metaphor for the believer), *al-burūj* (towers, constellations), *al-qadr* (destiny), *yaqdir* (allot, predestine), and *yuqaddir* (apportion, meditate, allocate).

2. Words that were new in terms of their etymological derivations, but which were taken from linguistic roots that were already familiar to the Arabs of that day. This category, which is larger than the first, includes words such as: *ātāhu* (he gave him), *malakūt* (kingdom, realm), *ṭāghūt* (powers of evil), *al-jāhiliyyah* (times of ignorance, that is, the pre-Islamic era), *ṣalawāt* (churches, houses of worship), *hādū* (followed the Jewish faith), *maqāmiʿ* (restraints, iron grips), *al-furqān* (what distinguishes

between truth and falsehood), *al-raqīm* (inscription), *marqūm* (recorded, registered, a record or register), *al-miḥrāb* (niche), *al-qaṣaṣ* (stories), *ghuzzā* (fighting), *al-muhtaẓir* (sheepfold), *al-anʿām* (cattle), *daḥḥāhā* (rolled it [the Earth]), *suʿur* (folly, madness), *tazāwar* (incline away from), *multaḥad* (refuge), *al-ʿādūn* (transgressors, those who go beyond proper limits), *rabbāniyyūn* (men of God), *qānitūn* (obedient), *al-munāfiqūn* (hypocrites), *ʿilliyyūn* (that mode most lofty), *shakūr* (deeply grateful [of a human being], responsive to gratitude [of God]), *al-ḥayawān* (true life), *al-sū'ā* (evil), *al-salsabīl* (a fountain in Paradise), *tilqā'* (towards), *wāʿadnā* (appointed, met with).

3. Words which, after passing beyond the phase of newness, into a phase of greater richness and interaction with daily life. This latter phase was one of stability and of widespread use and circulation. In such cases, the word or set of words concerned took on the characteristics of a "technical term" which had the power to convey a meaning far broader and more inclusive than the size of the term itself. Examples of such words or terms include: *mu'min* (believer), *kāfir* (unbeliever), *dhikr* (remembrance, the Islamic revelation), *masājid* (places of worship, literally, "places where one bows in worship"), *al-sāʿah* (the Day of Resurrection, literally, "the hour"), *ajr* (reward, especially in the afterlife), *al-taqwā* (God-consciousness, fear of God), *ḥasanah* (a good work, literally, "a beautiful something"), *sayyi'ah* (a bad work), *nikāḥ* (marriage), *al-ghayb* (the realm of the unseen), *al-shahādah* (the world of perception), *al-ṣalāh* (ritual prayer), *al-zakāh* (purifying alms), *al-īmān* (faith), *al-jihād* (struggle, striving), *al-shirk* (associating partners, *shurakā'*, with the one God), *al-ākhirah* (the afterlife), *al-qiyāmah* (the resurrection), and *al-nār* (hell-fire).

4. Words which had not been known or in circulation previously

among Arab speakers and whose roots were likewise unfamiliar to them, but which the Qur'an used in a linguistic context that enabled its listeners or readers to deduce their meanings. Most words belonging to this category are Arabized forms of words from other languages, particularly Farsi, Greek, Abyssinian, Nabatean, Syriac, Hebrew, and Coptic. Examples include: *ṣirāṭ* (straight way), *subḥānaka* (glory be to You [O God]), *abb* (grass), *qaswarah* (lion), *sijjīn* (a mode inescapable), *barzakh* (a barrier, a place in-between), *sijill* (record), *sijjīl* (stone and clay, hard as baked clay), *tannūr* (clay oven), *ḍīzā* (unfair), *qamṭarīr* (distressful, wrathful), *sundus* (silk), *istabraq* (brocade), *abārīq* (ewers, beakers), *al-qisṭ* (equity, just measure), *al-qisṭās* (full measure), *al-firdaws* (paradise), *mishkāh* (niche for a lamp), *ṭūbā* (happiness, blessedness), *qarāṭīs* (papers), *surādiq* (tent, pavilion), *ill* (pact, covenant, blood ties), *kursiyy* (chair, throne), *arā'ik* (couches), *jibt* (pit), and *yamm* (open sea).

5. Words which acquired their newness from the allegorical or figurative meaning with which the Qur'an invested them. In fact, most words in the world's various languages are born in this way. The Qur'an enriched the Arabic language with hundreds of such words, whose figurative meanings had theretofore been unknown among the Arabs. Such words include: *islām* (surrendering, relinquishing), *kufr* (covering, concealing [the truth, through unbelief]), *yatazakkā* (be purified by believing), *sidrah* (lote tree), *al-mīzān* (the scale [on which one's good and bad deeds will be "weighed" at the Judgment]), *ḥarth* (tilling, used in the sense of land and/or one's spouse, in a reference to sexual intimacy), *al-hudā* (guidance [along the path of truth]), *al-ḍalālah* (losing the way, error), *al-taqwā* (being wary, fearful, avoiding [God's wrath, through vigilance and good works]), *ummah* (a nation, a people, now used to refer to the Muslim nation in particular), *libās* (garment, clothing, used

metaphorically to speak of spiritual covering or protection), *muḥṣanāt* (virtuous women, literally "inaccessible"), *āyah* (sign, miracle; used to refer to the verses of the Qur'an), *al-awwāb* (one who returns, used to speak of God as the one who receives those who refer to Him), *al-ajal* (time appointed, death), *wāzirah* (a bearer of burdens, the human soul), *al-ḥāfirah* (the earth or ground), *al-sāhirah* (a state of complete awakeness), and *al-khunnas* (the hidden or unseen stars).

Nevertheless, as will be clear to readers, we have not relied on the sheer number of new words in the Qur'an for proof of the miraculousness of the Qur'an's language. This can be seen from the fact that of the 58 new linguistic phenomena that can be identified in the *Fātiḥah*, only five of these are new individual words, namely, *al-raḥmān*, *al-ʿalamīn*, *al-dīn* (in the sense of the Day of Judgment), *al-ṣirāṭ*, and *al-ḍāllīn*.

The Qur'an contains its own unique words, just as it contains its own distinctive patterns, constructions and linguistic links. However, we should be aware of the two significant differences between the place of Qur'anic words, on one hand, and Qur'anic patterns on the other. Unlike the Qur'anic patterns (*sabā'ik* سبائك), most of the single words in the Qur'an were not new to the Arabic language of the Prophet's day. Nor was it difficult or impossible to borrow and use such single words in the everyday Arabic language as it was to borrow and use the distinctive linguistic patterns found in the Qur'an. The Qur'anic linguistic patterns are, therefore, the Holy Book's "fingerprint," which no human linguistic pattern could ever replicate.

The New Words in Sūrah Al-Muddaththir

In *Sūrah al-Muddaththir*, which consists of 256 words and fills less than two pages, we can easily count up no fewer than 84 new words. In other words, nearly one-third of the words in this surah are new.

Here are examples of such words:

1. *Al-Rujz*: a new term used to refer to idols, or to torment.
2. *Al-Nāqūr*: a new term referring to the trumpet blown by the angel Isrāfīl as a sign of Judgement Day.
3. *Ṣaʿūdan*: a metaphorical image in which torment is likened to ascending a steep grade.
4. *Basar*: a new word meaning that the person's face grew dark.
5. *Lawwāḥah lil-bashar*: a phrase imbued with a new meaning, that is, changing the color of the skin (*al-basharah*), or, appearing clearly to human beings (*al-bashar*).
6. *Kafarū*: That is, they rejected the call to Islam. The original meaning of the verb *kafara* is to cover up or conceal; hence, the meaning is that they concealed the truth by closing their minds and hearts to it.
7. *Ūtū*: a new formulation and a new meaning, that is, "they were given."
8. *Rahīnah*: derived from the verb meaning to pawn or hold in pledge, the word *rahīnah* (pawn, hostage) is used to mean "accountable for."
9. *Salakakum*: a new form used in place of "brought you into."
10. *Saqar*: a new term meaning *Jahannam* (hell).
11. *Qaswarah*: a new term meaning "a lion," or archers, or bows.
12. *Al-Maghfirah*: a new word form referring to forgiveness.

The New Use of Particles in Sūrah Al-Muddaththir

In addition to the wealth of new vocabulary that fills *Sūrah al-Muddaththir*, it contains no fewer than 14 new uses of Arabic particles (*adawāt*). For example, the conjunction *fa* is placed in a different location than that which is customary in Arabic usage. *Fa* is normally placed between two verbs or two nouns, its function being to connect the second verb to the first verb, or the second noun to the first noun. Instead, we find that in three consecutive verses (verses 3–5), it is placed between the direct object (which heads the phrase rather than coming at the end of it), and its verb (which has been placed after the direct object rather than before it). Hence, verses 3–5 read as follows: *wa rabbaka fa kabbir* (literally, "and your Lord, then glorify"), *wa thiyābaka fa ṭahhir* ("and your garments, then purify"), and *wa al-rujza fahjur* ("and defilement, then shun"). In verse 7, we find it between a prepositional phrase and the verb with which the preposition is paired: *wa li rabbika faṣbir* ("and for your Lord, then wait in patience").

In addition, we find that in verses 16, 32, 53 and 54, the word *kallā*, which is normally used to express an emphatic "No!," is used in the sense of a reprimand, a deterrent, or perhaps in the sense of "truly."

In verses 19 and 20 – *fa qutila kayfa qaddara, thumma qutila kayfa qaddar* فَقُتِلَ كَيْفَ قَدَّرَ ثُمَّ قُتِلَ كَيْفَ قَدَّرَ (translated by Asad as, "and thus he destroys himself, the way he meditates: yea, he destroys himself, the way he meditates!" and by Abdullah Yusuf Ali as, "And woe to him! How he plotted! Yea, Woe to him; How he plotted!") – the interrogative particle *kayfa* is not used in an interrogative sense as it would be in non-Qur'anic Arabic. Nor is it used in an adverbial sense. Instead, it is used in a sense similar to that of a *ḥarf maṣdarī*,[15] in which case it can be interpreted together with the verb that follows it as the subject of the passive verb *qutila*. The meaning of the phrase would then be *qutila taqdīruhu*, which means literally, "his meditation (or plotting) was killed, that is, destroyed," or "may his meditation (or plotting) be killed, or destroyed." Still another interpretation would read *qutila jazā'a taqdīrihi*, "he was killed (or destroyed) – or, may he be killed (or destroyed) – in recompense for his meditation or plotting." If we adopt either of these interpretations, there is no basis for understanding the word *kayfa* as employed in these two verses either as an interrogative particle or as an adverb.

Furthermore, the particle *in* that occurs in verses 24 and 25 is used to convey a negation; hence, it is treated as an equivalent to *mā* or *laysa*. These two verses read: *Fa qāla in hādha illā siḥrun yu'thar. In hādha illā qawlu al-bashar*: فَقَالَ إِنْ هَذَا إِلاَّ سِحْرٌ يُؤْثَرُ إِنْ هَذَا إِلاَّ قَوْلُ الْبَشَرِ , "Then said he: 'This is nothing but (*in hādha illā*) magic, derived from of old. This is nothing but (*in hādha illā*) the word of a mortal!'" (Abdullah Yusuf Ali). This distinctive use of the particle *in*, which is as widespread and peculiar as the Qur'anic uses of *kāna* and of the phrase *mā zāla* (meaning "is still" when followed by a verb in the present tense), is found throughout the Qur'an. However, I have yet to find a single instance of it in pre-Islamic poetry.

The presence of no fewer than 84 new words in a small surah such as this, and one that was revealed very early in the Apostle's prophetic ministry, had the potential of causing a veritable cataclysm in the hearts and minds of those who heard it for the first time. It should come as no surprise, then, that after hearing the first 13 verses of *Sūrah Fuṣṣilat* (41), ʿUtbah ibn Rabīʿah, a leader of Quraysh with utter mastery of the Arabic language, came back to his people in a stupor, hardly able to comprehend a word he had heard. How much more of a cataclysm might we expect, then, if we consider the fact that, in addition to all the new words found in the Qur'an, it also contains scores of new constructions, expressions, linguistic patterns, metaphors, statements that admit of multiple interpretations, and elegantly concise turns of phrase, not to mention the new intellectual and cultural dimensions that intersect with the aforementioned linguistic and rhetorical developments?

RECONFIGURING THE LINGUISTIC UNIT

When the Qur'anic storm first blew in, it stirred up intense reactions commensurate with the momentousness of the Holy Book and all it had brought. However, as time passed, its impact on those who heard it began to diminish as subsequent generations grew accustomed to the Qur'anic language and, as a consequence, began losing the sense of awe that had been experienced by its first generation of hearers. The new Qur'anic linguistic phenomena no longer stopped people up short the way they had immediately following the book's descent. One of the phenomena that had been so disconcerting to the Qur'an's initial recipients was that of the *āyah*, or verse. The *āyah* represented a new concept that contrasted with both the clause (*jumlah*) – the basic linguistic unit of Arabic prose – and the stanza (*bayt*), which was the linguistic unit of Arabic poetry. The new linguistic unit represented by the *āyah* separated what Arabs had been accustomed to joining, and joined what they had they been accustomed to separating. Consequently, it opened a rift in Arabs' overall linguistic foundation which added new dimensions to the Arabic language and broadened its traditional horizons. Please read with me the following short passage from the beginning of *Sūrah Āl ᶜImrān* (3):

(v.3b) وَأَنزَلَ التَّوْرَاةَ وَالإِنجِيل

(v.4) مِن قَبْلُ هُدًى لِّلنَّاسِ وَأَنزَلَ الْفُرْقَانَ إِنَّ الَّذِينَ كَفَرُواْ بِآيَاتِ اللّهِ لَهُمْ عَذَابٌ شَدِيد

(v. 3b) *Wa anzala al-tawrāta wal-injīl* **(v. 4)** *min qablu hudan lil-nāsi wa anzala al-furqāna inna al-ladhīna kafarū bi āyāt illāhi lahum ᶜadhābun shadīd.*

(v. 3b) ...it is He who has bestowed from on high the Torah and the Gospel **(v. 4)** aforetime, as a guidance unto mankind, and it is He who has bestowed [upon man] the standard by which to discern the true from the false. Behold, as for those who are bent on denying God's messages – grievous suffering awaits them....

Note how verse 3 ends before the end of the sentence, that is, before the adverb "aforetime" (*min qablu*) that relates to the verbal phrase "bestowed from on high the Torah and the Gospel" (*wa anzala al-tawrāh wal-injīl*). Note also how the opposite occurs in verse 4, which extends beyond the end of the sentence that concludes with the words "unto mankind" (*lil-nās*) and the beginning of a new sentence ("and it is He who has bestowed..."). Verse 4 then continues beyond the sentence that ends with the words "…the standard by which to discern the true from the false" (*al-furqān*), and includes a new sentence that bears no grammatical connection to the sentence that precedes it: "Behold, as for those who are bent on denying God's messages – grievous suffering awaits them" (*inna al-ladhīna kafarū bi āyāt illāhi lahum ʿadhābun shadīd).*

Turning now to the first five verses of *Sūrah al-Rūm* (30), I have inserted diagonal lines in the places where, if this passage were divided up in accordance with our familiar linguistic traditions and units, we would expect one verse (*āyah*) to end and the next to begin:

> **(v. 1)** *Alif. Lām. Mīm.* **(v. 2)** *ghulibat al-rūm* **(v. 3)** *fī adnā al-arḍ // wa hum min baʿdi ghalabihim sa yaghlibūn* **(v. 4)** *fī biḍʿi sinīna // lillāhi al-amru min qablu wa min baʿdu // wa yawma'adhin yafraḥu al-mu'minūn* **(v. 5)** *bi naṣrillāhi // yanṣuru man yashā'u // wa huwa al-ʿazīz al-raḥīm.*

> **(v. 1)** *Alif. Lām. Mīm.* **(v. 2)** Defeated have been the Byzantines **(v. 3)** in the lands close-by; // yet it is they who, notwithstanding this their defeat, shall be victorious **(v. 4)** within a few years: // [for] with God rests all power of decision, first and last. // And on that day will the believers [too, have cause to] rejoice **(v. 5)** in God's succor: // [for] He gives succor to whomever He wills, // since He alone is Almighty, a Dispenser of grace.

As this passage should make clear, the Qur'anic divisions of these five verses – that is, the points at which one verse ends and the next verse begins – bear no relation to the ways in which we have been accustomed traditionally to dividing one sentence from another.

THE NEW SITUATION OF TRADITIONAL CONJUNCTIONS

This new scheme of divisions and connections is one of the most pervasive characteristics of the Qur'an's linguistic landscape. The most salient feature of this scheme is the omission of conjunctions such as *wāw*, *fā'*, *idh*, *inna*, *innamā*, and *qad*, and pronouns that appear as separate words (such as *huwa, hiya, hum*, etc.) from their traditional locations between sentences and clauses, a phenomenon that erases the language's generally recognized "regional boundaries." As an example of this phenomenon, let us read *Sūrah al-Raʿd* (13:33):

> *Afaman huwa qā'imun ʿalā kulli nafsin bi mā kasabat wa jaʿalū lillāhi shurakā'a qul sammūhum am tunabbi'ūnahu bi mā lā yaʿlamu fī al-arḍi am bi ẓāhirin min al-qawl bal zuyyina lilladhīna kafarū makruhum wa ṣuddū ʿan al-sabīli wa man yuḍlili Allāhu fa mā lahu min hādin.*

> Is, then, He who has every living being in His Almighty care, [dealing with each] according to what it deserves – [is, then, He like anything else that exists]? And yet, they ascribe to other beings a share in God's divinity! Say: "Give them any name [you please]: but do you [really think that you could] inform Him of anything on earth that He does not know—or [do you] but play with words?" Nay, goodly seems their false imagery to those who are bent on denying the truth, and so they are turned away from the [right] path: and he whom God lets go astray can never find any guide.

If we looked for the words omitted from this verse and restored them to the places where they would be located if the same meanings were expressed in keeping with our human linguistic conventions, the result would look something like this:

> *Afa* ***[hākadhā yakūnu]*** *man huwa qā'imun ʿalā kulli nafsin bi mā kasabat wa* ***[qad]*** *jaʿalū lillāhi shurakā'a* ***[fa]****qul* ***[lahum]*** *sammūhum* ***[idhan]*** *am* ***[taẓannūna annakum]*** *tunabbi'ūnahu bi mā lā yaʿlamu* ***[bi mā yūjad]*** *fī al-arḍi am* ***[inna hādha]*** *bi ẓāhirin min al-qawl* ***[minkum]*** *bal* ***[al-ḥaqqu annahu qad]*** *zuyyina lilladhīna kafarū makruhum wa ṣuddū ʿan al-sabīli…*

> أفَـ[هكذا يكون] مَن هو قـائمٌ على كلِّ نفْسٍ بما كسبَتْ و[قد] جعلوا للهِ شُركاءَ [فـ] قُلْ [لهم] سَمُّوهُم [إذن] أم [تظنّون أنّكم] تنبّئونه بما لا يعلمُ [بما يوجد] في الأرضِ أم [إنّ هذا] بظاهرٍ من القولِ [منكم] بل [الحقّ أنّه قد] زُيِّن للذين كفروا مكْرُهم وصَدّوا عن السبيل...

We see, then, that words have been omitted from at least ten places in this one verse alone.

Let us now try to bring to mind the conjunction that has disappeared from each of the highlighted spots in the following verses:

Wa qāla all-adhīna lā yaʿlamūna lawlā yukallimunā Allāhu aw ta'tīnā ***āyatun kadhā****lika qāla alladhīna min qablihim mithla qawli****him tashāba****hat qulūbu****hum qad*** *bayyannā al-āyāti li qawmin yūqinūn.* (*Sūrah al-Baqarah* 2:118)

And [only] those who are devoid of knowledge say, "Why does God not speak unto us, nor is a [miraculous] sign shown to us?" Even thus, like unto what they say, spoke those who lived before their time; their hearts are all alike. Indeed, We have made all the signs manifest unto people who are endowed with inner certainty.

Qul: innī ʿalā bayyinatin min rabbī ***wa kadh****dhabtum* ***bihi mā*** *ʿindī mā tastaʿjilūna* ***bihi in*** *al-ḥukmu illā lillā****hi ya****quṣṣu al-haqqa…* (*Sūrah al-Anʿām* 6:57)

Say: "Behold, I take my stand on a clear evidence from my Sustainer – and [so] it is to Him that you are giving the lie! Not in my power is that which [in your ignorance] you so hastily demand; judgment rests with none but God. He shall declare the truth…"

*Wa sakhkhar al-shamsa wa al-qam****ara kullun*** *yajrī li ajalin musamm****an yud****abbiru al-am****ra yuf****aṣṣilu al-āyāti laʿallakum bi liqā'i rabbikum tūqinūn.* (*Sūrah al-Raʿd* 13:2)

He [it is who] has made the sun and the moon subservient [to His laws], each running its course for a term set [by Him]. He governs all that exists. Clearly does He spell out these messages, so that you might be certain in your innermost that you are destined to meet your Sustainer [on Judgment Day].

This type of omission is not simply a new linguistic style that the Qur'an has added to the Arabic language. It is also a significant ideational and rhetorical addition, since it lends Qur'anic expression ethereal dimensions and imaginative subtleties that it would not have possessed otherwise. When numerous different types of omissions occur in a single verse, we find that the verse acquires an eloquence and a transparency over and above its original, basic meaning.

NEW INTER-WORD RELATIONSHIPS

All of the foregoing phenomena relate to what takes place between verses or sentences. So what about single words and their inter-relationships? The Qur'an produced a new warp and woof for inter-word connections. This new breed of connection had not been familiar in Arab culture prior to the appearance of the Qur'an, nor had it been familiar to other cultures, for that matter, before the emergence of new literary schools such as Symbolism and Surrealism in the modern era. Hence, it opened up new ideational and imaginative horizons that were now added to the text's original meaning.

For example, the fourth verse of the *Fātiḥah*, which reads, *māliki yawm al-dīn*, "Lord (or Master, or Owner) of the Day of Judgment," contains a link between words the mechanics of which the Arabs of the Prophet's day were unfamiliar. The Qur'an's first listeners undoubtedly sensed the difference between this verbal link and those to which they were accustomed and were accordingly shaken when they heard this verse for the first time. After all, their "linguistic laboratory" was as yet instinctual and primitive, since it lacked the advanced tools of research and analysis that are available to us today. The collocation of the words *mālik*, meaning "owner, master, lord," and *yawm*, meaning "day" was new to Arab and non-Arab alike at the time when the Qur'an first appeared. It was, and still is, customary for us to associate ownership (*mulk*) with concrete objects that can be possessed. We say, "the owner of the real estate," "the owner of the dirhems," "the owner of the land," "the owner of the car," "the owner of the ship," etc. But how can one speak of the owner of a day? Is time subject to being owned or possessed? Would banks and other financial institutions be willing to start opening accounts denominated in hours and days? The use of the phrase "owner of the day..." was thus a linguistic surprise with a very distinctive flavor for seventh-century Arabs. However, another surprise stood waiting just around the corner.

No sooner had they cleared this perplexing intersection than they were met by another traffic signal of a sort they would never have expected, and which loomed before them between the words *yawm* ("day") and *al-dīn* ("judgment"). Arabs and non-Arabs alike had been accustomed to pairing a word referring to a unit of time with a word describing some event that was to happen during the time specified. One might say, "a second of silence," "an hour of work," "the day of the battle," "the month of fasting," "the year of mourning," "the period of the war," "the age of awakening," etc. Before the Qur'an's first listeners understood the new meaning it conveyed in this verse, the word *dīn* did not refer to an event but, rather, to an abstract concept (religion). Hence, its collocation with a word referring to a period of time (*yawm*) was bound to cause them a mental traffic jam right on the heels of the one that had been triggered by the association of ownership (*mulk, mālik*) with a day (*yawm*). The unexpected turns in the road came thick and fast as the seventh-century Arabs made their way through this surah, and other surahs of the Qur'an as well. Consequently, their limited human tastes had to labor to take in the brief but intense "telegrams" that arrived one after another from Heaven, presenting them with a new string of linguistic links among sentences, phrases, and words. Through the confluence of all these new facets, the innovational revolution sparked by the Qur'an in both Arabic and other tongues went beyond language to the realm of the imagination in the form of graphic images, metaphorical uses, and rhetorical styles of expression.

THE NEW QUR'ANIC REPERTOIRE OF IMAGES

The same images were often repeated by pre-Islamic Arab poets. If an image used by one poet caught another poet's fancy, he would borrow it, reformulate it, and cast it in a new poetic mold; he might also use it in its original form. This pre-Islamic influence on the trajectory of Arabic poetry continued for many centuries thereafter, making its way into the works of some contemporary poets and writers, and possibly even into people's day-to-day conversation. The images employed were derived from the environment familiar to Arabs. Hence, the brave individual was a lion, the coward was an ostrich, the generous person was a sea, the niggard was a barren land, the resentful person was a camel, the glutton was an elephant, the somber, sedate individual was a mountain, the beautiful person was a sun or a moon, the refined person was a star, the base individual was a tent peg, the reckless or flighty person was a butterfly, the gentle, meek individual was a lamb, the stubborn, obstinate person was a dung beetle, the conceited person was a peacock, the wily, devious person was a fox, black hair was night, gray hair was daytime, the beloved's teeth were hailstones, her mouth was a ring or a daisy, her lips were carnelian, her cheeks were roses or apples, her teardrops were pearls, her fingertips were jujube fruits, her eyes were narcissus, her physique was a spear, her forehead was morning, her eyebrows were arrows, the locks that hung down over her temples were scorpions or scepters, etc.

As for the Holy Qur'an, it bypassed virtually all inherited images, removing them from its expressional stockpile and replacing them with its own illustrative vocabulary replete with fresh images. Although I have not undertaken an exhaustive survey of the images found in the Qur'an, I can state with almost complete certainty based on the verses I have examined in the course of this study that the expressional volcano that erupted out of the Qur'an was not limited to the creation of a colossal new illustrational stockpile which it added to our repertoire of metaphorical images. Rather, just as it had done with traditional linguistic patterns, the Qur'an abandoned, lock, stock and barrel, all the descriptive images recorded in the massive pre-Islamic poetic corpus, not one of which have I come across in a single *āyah*.

More important still is the fact that the Qur'an brought about a fundamental revolution in the artistic structure of the traditional linguistic image by introducing highly developed, varied, and seemingly unlikely connections between these images' component elements that were far ahead of their time. Whereas up to that time the images employed had been of limited quality and creativity, limited in number, composed of elements whose connecting links were limited in scope, and restricted almost entirely to poetry alone, the Qur'an broke out of these confines, ushering the Arabic imagination into a new era and a whole world of images that, with their wealth of new dimensions, inner dynamics and interconnections, had been theretofore unknown to Arabic poetry and prose alike.

The traditional rules drawn up and adhered to by rhetoricians divide metaphorical images into four elements: (1) the *mushabbah*, that is, the entity being likened to something else, (2) the *mushabbah bihi*, the "something else" to which the *mushabbah* is being likened, (3) the *adāt al-tashbīh*, that is, the word that points to the existence of a comparison or likeness (such as "like," "as," etc.), and (4) the *wajh shabah*, the point of similarity between the entity being likened to something else, and the "something else" to which it is likened. The image was then classified and categorized according to whether one or more of these four elements was explicitly mentioned or not. But when we attempt to subject the images found in the Qur'an to these traditional rules and classifications, we find that many of them refuse to fit into our time-honored categories. The following Qur'anic images, for example, cannot be analyzed based on conventional rules of rhetoric:

- *wa lakum fī al-qiṣāṣi ḥayāh* ("for in [the law of] just retribution...there is life for you" (*Sūrah al-Baqarah* 2:179).

- *ḍaʿufa al-ṭālibu wa al-maṭlūb* ("Weak indeed is the seeker, and [weak] the sought!") (*Sūrah al-Ḥajj* 22:73).
- *wa afʾidatuhum hawāʾun* ("and their hearts an abysmal void") (*Sūrah Ibrāhīm* 14:43).
- *wa yaqdhifūn bil-ghaybi min makānin baʿīd* ("...they (continually) cast (slanders) on the unseen from a position far off?") (*Sūrah Saba'* 34:53) (Abdullah Yusuf Ali's translation).

The Multi-dimensional Image

When the Qur'an was revealed, the Arabs of the Prophet's day had their first encounter with multi-dimensional images. When Arab rhetoricians began formulating the rules of Arabic rhetoric and analyzing metaphorical images into their component parts, they had no choice but to exclude Qur'anic images from their analyses because they did not conform to their rules, or, rather, because their limited human rules failed to contain or account for the dimensions displayed by the images in the Qur'an.

As for those who wanted to detract from Islam and the Qur'an, they viewed the peculiarity of the Qur'anic images and their non-conformity to traditional criteria as a weakness on the basis of which they believed they could attack the Muslims' creed. Ibn al-Rāwandī, the infamous freethinker whose present-day followers sing the praises of his innovativeness, rationality, and forward-looking notions, once commented to linguist and litterateur Ibn al-Aʿrabī on the passage of the Qur'an (16:112) according to which *adhāqahā Allāhu libās al-jūʿi wa al-khawfi*, which reads literally, "God caused it/them [the ungrateful city] to taste the garment of hunger and fear,"[16] saying, "Can a garment be tasted?" Ibn al-Aʿrabī replied, "All right then, you monkey: Suppose Muhammad wasn't a prophet. You certainly can't deny that he was an Arab!" For it was as though he [Ibn al-Rāwandī] was challenging the aforementioned verse by claiming that it would have been more appropriate for it to say, *fa kasāhāh Allāhu libās al-jūʿi* ("God clothed it/them with the garment of hunger") or *fa adhāqahā*

Allāhu ṭaʿm al-juʿi ("God caused it/them to taste the [bitterness] of hunger."[17]

The Hypothetical Image

The type of image I am referring to here is one that leaves it to our human imagination to complete it, because it places the *mushabbah*, or the entity being likened to something else, in juxtaposition with a *mushabbah bihi*, that is, the "something" to which it is being likened, which our ordinary human senses are incapable of grasping. Or it may liken something known to something which is unknown or which has never been experienced or observed by the listener/reader.

In one such image, the nature of which captured the interest of early rhetoricians, the Qur'an likens the fruit of the *zaqqūm* tree in Hell (translated by Asad as "the tree of deadly fruit," and by Yusuf Ali simply as "the Tree of *Zaqqūm*") to "satans' heads" (*Sūrah al-Ṣāffāt* 37:65). Since none of us has ever seen "satans," nor their heads, this image has the effect of letting our imaginations run wild in our attempts to envision the repulsiveness of this tree, which takes the form of the vilest creatures on the face of the earth. This type of image razes the barriers that a finite, logical, rational image places in the path of the human imagination, which now finds itself before endless horizons of conceptualizations and colors. Try now to enjoy with me, slowly and deeply, a number of Qur'anic images, taking them in with your imagination, your senses and your emotions:

> *Lā tudrikuhu al-abṣāru, wa huwa yudriku al-abṣār* (*Sūrah al-Anʿām* 6:103) ("No human vision can encompass Him, whereas He compasses all human vision").

> *Yawma tubaddalu al-arḍu ghayra al-arḍi wa al-samāwātu* (*Sūrah Ibrāhīm* 14:48) ("on the day when the earth shall be changed into another earth, as shall be the heavens").

Wa aṣbaḥa fu'ādu ummi mūsā fārighan (*Sūrah al-Qaṣaṣ* 28:10) (literally, "and the heart of Moses' mother became empty," translated by Asad as, "an aching void grew up in the heart of the mother of Moses").

Wa law annamā fī al-arḍi min shajaratin aqlāmun wa al-baḥru yamudduhu min baᶜdihi sabᶜatu abḥurin mā nafidat kalimātu Allāh (*Sūrah Luqmān* 31:27) ("And if all the trees on earth were pens, and the sea [were] ink, with seven [more] seas yet added to it, the words of God would not be exhausted…").

Wa al-arḍu jamīᶜan qabḍatuhu yawma al-qiyāmati wa al-samāwātu maṭwiyātun bi yamīnihi (*Sūrah al-Zumar* 39:67) ("…the whole of the earth will be as a [mere] handful to Him on Resurrection Day, and the heavens will be rolled up in His right hand").

Fa idhā inshaqqat al-samā'u fa kānat wardatan kal-dihāni (*Sūrah al-Raḥmān* 55:37) ("And when the sky is rent asunder and becomes red like [burning] oil").

Wa laqad zayyanā al-samā' al-dunyā bi maṣābīḥa wa jaᶜalnāhā rujūman lil-shayāṭīn (*Sūrah al-Mulk* 67:5) ("And, indeed, We have adorned the skies nearest to the earth with lights, and have made them the object of futile guesses for the evil ones" [Asad]; or, "And we have, (from of old), adorned the lowest heaven with Lamps, and We have made such (Lamps) (as) missiles to drive away the Evil Ones" [Abdullah Yusuf Ali]).

Wa in yakādu alladhīna kafarū la yuzliqūnaka bi abṣārihim (*Sūrah al-Qalam* 68:51) ("And the Unbelievers would almost trip thee up with their eyes …" [Abdullah Yusuf Ali]).

The Types of Images Found in Surah Al-Muddaththir (74)

If we look once more at *Sūrah al-Muddaththir*, we find that it contains no fewer than 31 images of the aforementioned types. It should be borne in mind that these Qur'anic images were entirely new to the

Image	English translation	Verse	Rhetorical classification
wa thiyābaka fa ṭahhir	"And thine inner self [or, thy garments] purify!"	4	Metaphor (the word "garments" is used to refer to the person's inner self)
sa urhiquhu ṣaʿūdan	"I shall constrain him to endure a painful uphill climb!"	17	Metonymy or allusion to intense suffering, the nature of which is unspecified
adbara wa istakbara	"he turns his back [on Our message] and glories in his arrogance"	23	Metonymy or allusion, with the phrase "turns his back" being likened to the act of denial or rejection
kafarū	"are bent on denying the truth"	31	A metaphor in which denial of the truth is likened to the act of covering (the verb *kafara* in its origin means to cover or conceal) the mind
yuḍillu Allāhu man yashā'u	"God lets go astray him that wills [to go astray]"	31	A simile in which the act of inducing or allowing unbelief is likened to leading someone onto the wrong path.
yahdī man yashā'u	"and guides aright him that wills [to be guided]"	31	A simile in which the act of inducing or enabling belief is likened to guiding someone along the right path
wa al-ṣubḥi idhā asfara	"And by the dawn as it shineth forth"	34	A simile in which dawn is likened to the act of uncovering the night (the word *asfara* meaning to uncover or reveal)
kullu nafsin bi mā kasabat rahīnah	"every human being will be held in pledge for whatever [evil] he has wrought"	38	A simile in which the human being in likened to someone imprisoned behind the bars of the actions he has committed
aṣḥāb al-yamīn	"those who shall have attained to righteousness" (literally, "the companions of the right")	39	A metonym or allusion to those who inhabit paradise
al-taqwā	"God-consciousness"	56	An allusion to or symbol of the fear of God's chastiment (the noun *al-taqwā* is derived from the root t–q–y, meaning to fear or beware of), which manifests itself in righteous action

Table 4: Rhetorical Classifications of Images Employed in *Sūrah al-Muddaththir*

Arabs of the Prophet's day, including both those that were based on elements that had been known prior to Islam, and those that went beyond them. It should also be remembered that the rhetorical classification we have assigned to each of these images does not necessarily represent the final, or only, categorization, since, as we have had occasion to note, many images found in the Qur'an defy categorization based on the boundaries and criteria defined by scholars of Arabic rhetoric. Such images include those in *Table 4*.

AL-ILTIFĀT: A LINGUISTIC ART UNIQUE TO THE QUR'AN

Rhetoricians have often discussed a linguistic phenomenon which they classify under the rubric of semantics and which has come to be known as *iltifāt*, or sudden transition. In a literary context, *iltifāt* refers to an unexpected shift on the part of the writer or speaker from one mode of address to another. For example, there may be a sudden shift from the third person (he, she, they) to the second person (you), or from the second person (you) to the first person (I, we), or from the singular to the plural. Some rhetoricians might also include a shift from past tense, to present tense, to the imperative, from a noun to a verb, and so on. In the following verse, for example, we have a shift from singular to plural: *balā man aslama wajhahu lillāhi wa huwa muḥsinun fa lahu ajruhu ʿinda rabbihi wa lā khawfun ʿalayhim wa lā hum yaḥzanūn*, "Yea, indeed: everyone who surrenders **his** whole being unto God, and **is** a doer of good withal, shall have **his** reward with **his** Sustainer; and they will **have** no fear, and neither shall **they** grieve" (*Sūrah al-Baqarah* 2:112). Whereas the verse begins with the use of the third person singular (everyone, his), it concludes with the use of the third person plural (they), although the individuals being spoken of in both parts of the verse are the same.

When citing examples of this phenomenon, rhetoricians have unfortunately not distinguished between verses from the Qur'an and lines from pre-Islamic poetry. Granted, they have cited more Qur'anic verses in illustration of *iltifāt* than they have lines of pre-Islamic poetry, which in itself is an indirect admission of the Qur'an's priority in this connection. Academically speaking, however, such lines of poetry are not worthy to be placed on a par with verses from the Qur'an as illustrations of this phenomenon. In his book *Miftāḥ al-ʿUlūm*, al-Sakākī cites the following two lines of poetry by ʿAlqamah al-Faḥl (d. 603 CE)[18] in his chapter on *iltifāt*:

Ṭaḥā bika qalbun fī al-ḥisāni ṭarūbu طحا بكَ قلبٌ في الحِسانِ طروبُ	*Buʿayda al-shabābi ʿaṣra ḥāna mashību* بُعَيدَ الشبابِ عصرَ حانَ مَشيبُ
Your joyful heart has lost its senses over the beautiful women	Though youth is gone and old age has set in
Ukallifunī Laylā wa qad shaṭṭa walyuhā يكلّفُني ليلَى وقد شَطَّ وَلْيُها	*Wa ʿādat ʿawādin baynanā wa khuṭūbu* وعادتْ عَوادٍ بيننا وخُطوبُ
He [my heart] burdens me to draw near Layla now that she has departed	And preoccupations, hindrances and afflictions have come between us

My question is: Can we find any type of *iltifāt* in these lines, or even anything remotely related to it? Most, if not all, rhetoricians have insisted that we can. In fact however, these lines contain nothing but an ordinary conversation of the sort one has with oneself. As is customary for poets, as well as for any one of us, ʿAlqamah projects himself as another person who addresses him as "you," and he proceeds to have a conversation with himself as though he were someone else sitting across from him. He then returns to himself and begins speaking in the first person ("I"). How many times have we all spoken to ourselves in this way? I may say, "What's happened to you, Bassam? I'm not comfortable with what you're doing to yourself. So, then, I'll go back on my decision. Yes, that would be better for you, Bassam."

In the course of my monologue, I went back and forth several times between speaking to myself in the second person ("you") and using the first person ("I"). But could I rightfully refer to this process as *iltifāt*? And would I be entitled to place it side by side with the Qur'anic art known by this name?

Iltifāt in the Holy Qur'an is an entirely new art that was unknown to pre-Islamic Arabic literature, and that has been unknown to it ever since. To this day it is a phenomenon that remains inaccessible to human writers, and I personally know of nothing similar to it in any other language. Nor is it something that simply happens accidentally here and there. Rather, it constitutes a consistent rhetorical phenomenon in which the Qur'an alone specializes. When I refer to *iltifāt* as a "phenomenon," I use this word to emphasize the frequency with which various forms of this art manifest themselves throughout the Qur'anic text. Also note, an extraordinary feature of the shifting use of pronouns is that reader attention is constantly engaged in a flow of energy which requires the brain to think, moving from I, we, you, he, they, at speed, directing the mind to intellectually engage and focus. As we will see shortly, the pronoun referring to God shifts no fewer than six times between "he" (*huwa*), "I" (*anā*), and "we" (*naḥnu*) in the first three verses of *Sūrah al-Isrā'* (17:1-3):

> *Subḥāna alladhī asrā bi ᶜabdihi laylan min al-masjidi al-ḥarāmi ilā al-masjidi al-aqṣā alladhī bāraknā ḥawlahu li nuriyahu min āyātinā innahu huwa al-samīᶜu al-baṣīr. Wa ātaynā mūsā al-kitāba wa jaᶜalnāhu hudan li banī isrā'īla allā tattakhidhū min dūnī wakīlan. Dhurriyata man ḥamalnā maᶜa nūḥin innahu kāna ᶜabdan shakūran.*

> Limitless in His glory is He who transported His servant by night from the Inviolable House of Worship [at Mecca] to the Remote House of Worship [at Jerusalem] – the environs of which We had blessed – so that We might show him some of Our symbols: for, verily, He alone is All-Hearing and All-Seeing. And [thus, too] We vouchsafed revelation unto Moses, and

> made it a [source of] guidance for the children of Israel, [commanding them:] "Do not ascribe to any but Me the power to determine your fate. O you descendants of those whom We caused to be borne [in the ark] with Noah! Behold, he was a most grateful servant [of Ours]!" (*Sūrah al-Isrā'* 17:1-3)

Iltifāt in Relation to Time

There are numerous types of Qur'anic *iltifāt*, one of which involves temporal overlap such that the past, the present and the future are merged into one. Here we are dealing with divine dimensions of place and time that refuse to be bound by our human definitions. Qur'anic expressions and phrases often flit back and forth among these three human temporal spheres without regard for our earthly norms and boundaries; they free themselves from earthly restraints and defy the boundaries we have drawn for them in our finite minds. The following verses from the Qur'an will give us a sense of the way in which temporal boundaries are blurred and intertwined:

> *Wa law tarā idh* ***wuqifū*** *ʿalā al-nār fa* ***qālū*** *yā laytanā nuraddu wa lā nukadhdhiba bi āyāti rabbinā*: "If thou couldst but see [them] when they **were exposed** to the fire **saying**, 'Oh, would that we are brought back [to life]: then we would not deny our Sustainer's messages..." (*Sūrah al-Anʿām* 6:27)

Even though the passage is speaking about the future Day of Judgment, it uses the past tense to describe these events.

> *Wa kadhālika* ***nuri*** *ibrāhīma malakūta al-samāwāti wa al-arḍi*: "And thus We **give** Abraham [his first] insight into [God's] mighty dominion over the heavens and the earth..." (*Sūrah al-Anʿām* 6:75)

The passage is describing a past action of God with the use of the present tense.

> *Wa **yaṣnaᶜu** al-fulka wa kullamā **marra** ᶜalayhi mala'un min qawmihi **sakhirū** minhu:* "And so [Noah] sets himself to building the ark; and every time the great ones of his people passed by him, they scoffed at him." (*Sūrah Hūd* 11:38)

Noah's action in the past is described with the use of a verb in the present tense, while the accompanying actions of others are described using the past tense.

Iltifāt in the Accusative Case

However, of the various types of Qur'anic *iltifāt*, the one that is most remarkable and that most merits our attention is what I might term "grammatical *iltifāt*." This type of *iltifāt* manifests itself most particularly in situations in which the accusative case is used in an unexpected manner or location. Situations such as these have bewildered untold numbers of grammarians, who have labored, as they have in relation to all Qur'anic linguistic phenomena that refuse to conform to their inadequate human rules, to come up with grammatical justifications for them even if this required them at times to move away from the actual meaning of the verse in question. So, until such time as grammarians arrive – if they ever do – at a fixed grammatical formulation for this type of accusative, I propose that, instead of losing ourselves in grammatical labyrinths, we classify this phenomenon simply as "a Qur'anic accusative," or "an *iltifāt*-based accusative." As for the skeptical Orientalists who claim that these unexpected and unorthodox Qur'anic uses of the accusative are "mistakes," plain and simple, their claims, and the claims of any other skeptic, for that matter, can be disproved by the following considerations:

(1) The Qur'an predates Arabic grammatical rules. In fact, it was the Qur'an that served to motivate grammarians, linguists and rhetoricians to lay down the grammatical rules we have today, and had it not been for the Qur'an, these scholars would not have been able to

formulate such rules during that early phase in the life of the Arabic language. In sum, the Qur'an is what stands watch over the rules of Arabic grammar, not the rules of Arabic grammar that stand watch over the Qur'an.

(2) If Prophet Muhammad, to whom our skeptical Orientalist friends attribute authorship of the Qur'an, made mistakes in the Book, then the question remains why did he not make mistakes in his everyday conversation as recorded in the hadiths that have come down to us? Would he have been more careful to correct the errors in his everyday conversations than he was in the Qur'an, despite the fact that the sayings attributed to him are tens of times greater in volume than the Qur'an, and although the Prophetic hadiths that have come down to us are the outcome of the spontaneous, everyday language he spoke with the people around him? Does it make any sense to claim that when he spoke extemporaneously his language was flawless whereas, when he went into seclusion and, far from people's watchful eyes, labored to compose a text that he would soon thereafter attribute to his God, his language was filled with errors?

(3) If there were indeed errors in the Qur'an, would not the Companions who were well-versed in poetry and the intricacies of eloquent speech have been capable of correcting these errors, thereby ensuring that the Qur'an would reach us error-free? Even more importantly, wouldn't such errors have alienated these Companions from this new religion, whose deity had failed to master the simplest rules of writing and composition?

(4) Assuming for the sake of argument that there are, in fact, errors in the Qur'an, it should be borne in mind that many instances of grammatical *iltifāt* in the Qur'an involve placing a word in the accusative case (such as making the subject of a nominal sentence accusative, as in *al-shams**a** mushriqah*) – with a *fatḥah* – when it would normally be

with a *ḍammah*, and that errors of this sort are so obvious that even a beginner in the Arabic language would never commit them. The following are examples of this use of the accusative case:

- *Khālidīna fīhā abadan waᶜda Allāhi haqqan*: "to dwell therein forever. God's promise is the truth" (*Sūrah al-Nisā'* 4:122; Abdullah Yusuf Ali). The word "promise" (*waᶜd*) is in the accusative case rather than the nominative although it is the subject of the sentence, "God's promise is the truth."

- *Fa innahu rijsun aw fisq**an** uhilla li ghayri Allāhi bihi*: "for that, behold, is loathsome – or a sinful offering over which any name other than God's has been invoked" (*Sūrah al-Anᶜām* 6:145). The word *fisq,* translated here as "a sinful offering" is placed in the accusative case even though the noun *rijs*, "loathsome," is in the nominative, and both words are part of the same noun phrase.

- *Walaqad jā'at rusulunā ibrāhīma bil-bushrā qālū salām**an** qāla salām**un***: "There came our messengers to Abraham with glad tidings. They said, 'Peace!' He answered, 'Peace!'"(Abdullah Yusuf Ali) (*Sūrah Hūd* 11:69). The first instance of the word *salām* ("peace") is in the accusative case while the second is in the nominative case even though, grammatically speaking, the constructions are exactly the same.

- *Dhālika ᶜīsā ibnu maryama qawl**a** al-ḥaqq*: "Such was, in the words of truth, Jesus the son of Mary" (Asad) or, "Such(was) Jesus the son of Mary: (it is) a statement of truth" (Ali) (*Sūrah Maryam* 19:34). The word *qawl* would normally be expected to be in the nominative case, but is in the accusative case instead.

- *Inna hādhihi ummat**u**kum ummat**an** wāḥidatan*: "Verily, [O you who believe in Me,] this community of yours is one single community"

(*Sūrah al-Anbiyā'* 21:92). As the predicate of a nominal sentence, the phrase "one single community" (*ummah wāḥidah*) would normally be in the nominative, but is in the accusative instead.

- *Wa mā jaᶜala ᶜalaykum fī al-dīni min ḥarajin millat**a** abīkum ibrāhīm*: "[He] has laid no hardship on you in [anything that pertains to] religion, [and made you follow] the creed of your forefather Abraham" (Asad) or, "…it is the cult of your father Abraham" (Ali) (*Sūrah al-Ḥajj* 22:78). The word *millah* (creed or cult) might be expected to be in the nominative case, but is in the accusative. Note how Asad interpolates a phrase that would "explain" why it is in the accusative here.

- *Salām**un** qawl**an** min rabbin raḥīm*: "'Peace!' – a word (of salutation) from a Lord Most Merciful" (Ali) (*Sūrah Yā Sīn* 36:58). The word *qawl* would be expected to be in the nominative case rather than the accusative. The same is true for the words underlined in the remaining passages quoted below.

- *Kallā innahā laẓā nazzāᶜat**an** lil-shawā*: "Verily, all [that awaits him] is a raging flame, *tearing away* at his skin" (*Sūrah al-Maᶜārij* 70:15-16).

- *Wa mizājuhu min tasnīm ᶜayn**an** yashrabu biha al-muqarrabūn*: "for it is composed of all that is most exalting – a source [of bliss] whereof those who are drawn close unto God shall drink" (*Sūrah al-Muṭaffifīn* 83:27–28).

- *Sa yaṣlā nāran dhāta lahabin wamra'atuhu ḥammālat**a** al-ḥaṭab*: "he shall have to endure a fire fiercely glowing, together with his wife, that carrier of evil tales" (*Sūrah al-Masad* 111:3–4).

Lastly, the presence of at least fifteen instances of *iltifāt* of various types in a small, early surah such as *al-Muddaththir* is clear evidence of the magnitude and significance of *iltifāt* among the various new linguistic phenomena found in the Qur'an. It also points to the magnitude of the linguistic and rhetorical shock that was experienced by the early Arabs as they heard the words of the revelation for the first time.

OPEN LANGUAGE

The Qur'an surprised the Arabs of the Prophet's day with a new type of language possessed of many facets that were in complete harmony with each other. This flexible divine language had the capacity to remain alive down the ages in such a way that people could discover within it meanings that their forebears had not discerned because the realities of their particular era or generation and the limited knowledge available to them had prevented them from seeing them. As a consequence, the people of every generation and, possibly, of every land and culture, understand this language in keeping with their own way of thinking, the discoveries they have made, and the knowledge available to them. I have to confess that it took me a long time to appreciate the wisdom behind ʿUmar ibn al-Khaṭṭāb's refusal to allow people to interpret the Qur'an or ask about its meanings. ʿUmar was so adamant on this point that he went so far as to have people beaten, flogged and imprisoned for violating this prohibition. Abū al-ʿAbbās related the following, "We were in the presence of ʿUmar ibn al-Khaṭṭāb (may God be pleased with him) when a man approached him and said, 'O Commander of the Faithful, what does the phrase *al-jawāri al-kunnas* (*Sūrah al-Takwīr* 81:16) refer to?' In response, ʿUmar punctured the man's turban and sent it flying off his head. Then he said, 'Are you a Kharijite? By the One who holds ʿUmar ibn al-Khaṭṭāb's life in His hands, if you hadn't had something covering your head just now, I would have cut it off!'"[19]

Seen from our limited perspective, an interpretation of the Qur'an coming from that period of history – the period during which the Prophet and his Companions lived – would be a treasure trove filled with golden keys to the world of linguistic mysteries that lie hidden within the Qur'an. However, from the perspective of a far-sighted, discerning man like ʿUmar, it would have meant shutting down people's minds at a later time, since it would have limited their ability to engage in their own interpretative efforts and their own discoveries of the Qur'an's mysteries and miracles. After all, as the Prophet Muhammad himself said, the Qur'an is a book whose wonders never cease (*lā tanqaḍī ʿajā'ibuhu*). Who, then, even in the second century AH, would have dared suggest a new interpretation of this or that verse if a different interpretation had been established in the first century AH, and in the era of an illustrious Companion the likes of ʿUmar? And how much more hesitant would such a person be if he knew that ʿUmar had heard of such an interpretation but remained silent about it?

The innumerable discoveries being made today of the Qur'an's miraculous insights into matters pertaining to scientific knowledge have to do with facts that had been previously unknown to humankind and which, for this reason, had remained concealed for long centuries beneath the wings of the open or multifaceted language of which we speak. Hence, such discoveries are simply one fruit of this particular linguistic feature of the Book of God. They are likewise a fruit of the noble Companions' having preserved the Qur'an without allowing interpretations of it to be recorded for posterity. "Open" or multifaceted words or expressions are found in many of the verses referred to as *mutashābih* (allegorical – see *Sūrah Āl ʿImrān* 3:7). However, they are not to be found in those referred to as *muḥkam* (basic or fundamental, of established meaning, clear in and of themselves), which have to do with the Qur'an's fundamental teachings about the oneness of God. Commentators might easily differ, for example, over the meaning of the multifaceted term *al-ṣamad* – variously translated as, "the Eternal, the Uncaused Cause of all that exists" (Asad), and "the Eternal, Absolute" (Abdullah Yusuf Ali) – in *Sūrah al-Ikhlāṣ* (112), since its potential meanings, however varied they happen to be, do not depart from the essence of monotheism. By contrast, however, there is no place for differences of opinion or interpretation in relation to the expressions that precede and follow *al-ṣamad*, such as *aḥad* ("the One God," "the One and Only"), *lam yalid* ("He begets not") and *lam yūlad* ("and neither is He begotten"), since these go to the heart of monotheism, and there is no room here for debate or differing interpretations regardless of differences in time, place and culture.

The phrase *Allāhu akbar* provides a ready example of what we mean by "open language." This expression has generally been translated into English either as "God is great," or "God is the greatest." However, neither of these statements is a precise translation of *Allāhu akbar*, since the word *akbar* translates into English as "greater." Hence, the correct translation of *Allāhu akbar* is, "God is greater." Despite the fact that this breaks with linguistic conventions that require the comparative adjective to be followed by the particle *min*, "than," Islam has left this expression open in order to allow the person uttering it to imagine whatever ending best fits his or her circumstances. "God is greater..." than everything: than any sorrow, than any joy, than any worry, than any lust, passion or desire, than any oppressor, etc. If the expression used were *Allāhu al-akbar* ("God is the greatest"), or *Allāhu al-kabir* ("God is the great One"), the expression would become self-contained rather than open-ended and, as a result, it would no longer leave any maneuvering room for our imagination or our thoughts. Familiarity has caused us to lose our ability to take hold of the most beautiful aspects of this expression's newness, singularity and openness. We have come to repeat it as though it meant nothing more than "God is great," and this is what has given rise to the distorted, erroneous translations of it into other languages.

The best measure of the richness and multidimensionality of a word or expression is the number of inflections it can be given. The more possible ways there are to inflect (*iʿrāb*) a word or expression, the more luminous it is, the more meanings it communicates, and the more nuanced, suggestive and colorful it is. The Qur'an surpassed both the poetry and the prose of its day, surprising seventh-century Arabs with a language that could respond to changing times, new events and discoveries, differing personalities, and the evolution of human thought, culture, and knowledge. As a result people take from the Qur'an that which their particular understanding and culture are capable of accommodating, and what suits their particular era, location, environment, mentality and needs. However, the contents of the Qur'an itself, however disparate and varied the conditions to which the Book is responding, remain self-consistent throughout. The abundant supply of multifaceted words and expressions in the Qur'an has thus given the Arabs the opportunity to enrich their literature and poetry beyond measure.

It is easy to find this type of open language in the texts of previously revealed scriptures, that is, the Old Testament (*al-tawrāh*) and the New Testament (*al-injīl*). However, we are unable to arrive at a sound, objective judgment concerning such texts, because most of the texts that we have available to us are narrated by human beings or, at best, by prophets, and only rarely do we encounter texts in which God speaks directly (i.e. in odd verses here and there in the Old Testament). Hence for the most part these texts are not God's *ipsissima verba*: the very language of Heaven. Rather, they are, at best, an interpretation of God's words. Nor do we possess these texts in the languages in which they were originally revealed. Hence, no matter how accurate the available translation happens to be, it remains no more than a personal interpretation that expresses, in a limited way, the translator's point of view on what he or she is translating. Add to this the fact that translations are often muddled, especially if the translator is so thorough, objective and honest that he or she cannot in good conscience render the obscure parts of the text into precise, clear language, as a result of which he or she resorts to the use of a confusing style that imbues the translation with an opacity or vagueness that gives it the appearance of what we might think of as open language when, in fact, it is simply unclear. And lastly, we have the difficulty that grammatical, verbal and cultural differences among languages cause for translators as they attempt to transfer meanings from one language to another language which has its own varied rules, cultural associations, and conventions.

We would be justified, for example, in hesitating to class an obscure Old Testament phrase such as "Thou ordained strength because of thine enemies" (Psalms 8:2), and whose Arabic translation reads, *assasta ḥamdan bi sababi aḍḍādika* أسّست حمداً بسبب أضدادِكَ [20] as an instance of open language, especially in view of the fact that the English translation of the phrase is more unequivocal than its Arabic counterpart. My own translation of the phrase, which, like all translations, has its drawbacks, reads *la qad aksabaka aʿdā'uka quwwatan* ("Thine enemies have increased Thy strength"), while another Arabic translation reads, *taʿazzazta fī wajhi khuṣūmika* تعزّزتَ في وجهِ خصومكَ [21] ("Thou hast been strengthened in the face of Thine enemies"), which is less ambiguous than the Arabic translation cited earlier, but not as clear as the English translation. We do not face this problem with the Qur'an, in which God speaks in the first person from beginning to end. Moreover, we have the Qur'an in its original language, as a result of which we are not obliged to pass through one or more mediary languages in order to arrive at its meaning as we are when dealing with other revealed scriptures.

Instances of "Open Language" in Sūrah Al-Muddaththir

We have relied thus far on *Sūrah al-Muddaththir* (74) in our analytical study of the various new linguistic phenomena to be found in the Qur'an. This surah presents us with numerous instances of innovative language that have sparked controversy among commentators, linguists and grammarians, and which lend themselves readily to multiple interpretations and grammatical analyses. If, moreover, we take into account the numerous different readings of the Qur'an recognized down the centuries as valid, we emerge with no fewer than 29 instances of what I am terming "open" words or expressions. *Table* 5 lists some of them with only one of the meanings suggested for each.

"Open" word or expression	English translation (Muhammad Asad)	Verse
qum fa andhir	"Arise and warn"	2
wa rabbaka fa kabbir	"and thy Sustainer's greatness glorify"	3
wa al-rujza fahjur	"And all abomination shun!"	5
wa lā tamnun tastakthir	"and do not through giving seek thyself to gain"	6
wa banīna shuhūda	"and children as [love's] witnesses"	13
wa mahhadtu lahu tamhīda	"To whom I made (life) smooth and comfortable!"	14
kallā	"verily…"	16
lawwāḥatun lil-bashar	"making [all truth] visible to mortal man"	29
li man shā'a minkum an yataqaddama aw yata'akhkhar	"to everyone of you, whether he chooses to come forward or to hang back!"	37
illā aṣḥāb al-yamīn	"save only those who shall have attained to righteousness"	39
nakhūḍu maʿa al-khāiḍʿīn	"we were wont to indulge in sinning together with all [the others] who indulged in it"	45
an yu'tā ṣuḥufan munashsharah	"to have been given revelations unfolded"	52
huwa ahlu al-taqwā	"the Fount of all God-consciousness"	56

Table 5: Depicting some "open" words or expressions found in *Sūrah al-Muddaththir*

If we pause and reflect on each of these words or phrases, we can discern for ourselves the numerous dimensions and nuances that each of them conveys. Take, for example, the first phrase, *qum fa andhir*, translated by Asad as "Arise and warn." The command *qum* could convey a number of different meanings. It could mean, "Rise," "Get up," "Move," "Get to work," or "Prepare yourself." As for the command *andhir*, it could mean "deliver the message," "warn of the impending hour of judgment," "warn of chastisement in this earthly life," or "warn of spending eternity in hell-fire." Similarly, the final phrase, *huwa ahlu al-taqwā*, translated by Asad as "the Fount of all God-consciousness," is filled with varied potential significations. The noun *ahlu* can refer to an entity's owner, its giver, someone who is worthy of it, or its authoritative source. As for the noun *al-taqwā*, its semantic range includes wariness or the propensity to fear and avoid something, such as the avoidance of God's chastisement on the Day of Judgment by virtue of our faith in Him. It can also refer to prevention or protection, as in God's protection of people from this chastisement when they place their faith in Him, or His protection of them from the evils of this earthly realm.

The wealth of open language found in *Sūrah al-Muddaththir* gives us an idea of the extent to which this type of language, on the level of both individual words and expressions, dominates the language of the Qur'an in all other surahs as well. At the same time, it should be stressed that the openness of this language does not mean that there is a dangerous breach in the Qur'an that would enable those with an axe to grind to distort its message. Such people have been attempting to do this very thing for ages, in fact, and they continue to do so. Rather, this distinctive feature enriches the meanings conveyed by the Qur'an, lending them greater vitality and ingenuity as the centuries pass, as human knowledge evolves, and as human environments and cultures develop and change.

The Various Qur'anic Readings and Open Language

The existence of recognized variant readings of the Qur'an[22] is one of the most remarkable illustrations we have of open language. It is, in fact, a feature that has been associated with no other book in the history of humankind. Orientalists and others of their ilk have aroused controversy over this miraculous aspect of the Qur'an's language, writing lengthy studies on it and offering generous grants for such research in the hope of finding justifications for their skepticism and undermining the Qur'an's credibility and authority. However, never once have they paused to reflect honestly on their own scientific approaches, and from which we Easterners have learned so much. If they did, they would have to acknowledge that the seven variant Qur'anic readings are simply one more miraculous aspect of this remarkable book's language.

Have you ever heard of there being several books in one, or a text that can be read in more than one way, or be seen to convey more than one meaning, yet without there being any contradiction or inconsistency among these meanings? It is not a matter of disagreement among Muslims. Rather, it is a matter of there being varied ways of reading the Qur'an that were revealed from on high in order to enrich the Qur'an's language and message, facilitate its reading, and highlight the open nature of its language in such a way that it can harmonize with changing times and places. The seven readings of the Qur'an, then, represent an additional feature that is unique to this book alone. If there is any difference among linguists or readers regarding these readings, it is simply a matter of "who prefers which," since seven of them in particular were divinely revealed:

> ʿUmar ibn al-Khaṭṭāb (may God be pleased with him) said, "One day during the lifetime of the Messenger of God (SAW) I heard Hishām ibn Ḥakīm reciting *Sūrah al-Furqān* (25). As I listened to him, I noticed that he was reciting it using numerous pronunciations that I had never heard the Messenger of God use. I nearly interrupted him in the middle of his prayer. However, I thought better of it and waited until he had finished. Then I grabbed him by the collar of his robe and said, 'Who taught you the surah I just heard you reciting?' He replied, 'The Messenger of God (SAW) taught me to recite it

> this way.' 'You're lying,' I said. 'I swear to God that the Apostle (SAW) taught me to recite it in another way!' Then I led him off to the Messenger of God (SAW) and said, 'O Messenger of God, I heard this man reciting *Sūrah al-Furqān* in a way that was different than the way you taught me.' The Messenger of God (SAW) replied, 'Let him go, ʿUmar.' Then, speaking to Hishām, he said. 'Recite, Hishām.' Hishām recited the surah in the way I had heard him recite it during his prayer. The Messenger of God (SAW) then said, 'This is the way it was revealed.' Then he turned to me and said, 'Recite, ʿUmar.' So I recited the surah in the way he had taught me to, and he said, 'This is the way it was revealed. This Qur'an was revealed with seven different pronunciations (literally, "letters"), so recite it using whichever of them is easiest for you.'"[23]

It is important to note here that the various readings of the Qur'an – of which there happen to be seven because the number of reciters with whom the chains of narrators on which we base these readings end were seven in number – are not to be confused with the "seven letters" (*al-ḥurūf al-sabʿah*) mentioned in the Prophetic hadith just cited, and which refer to the local dialects and differing pronunciations associated with the educated and the illiterate, youths and the elderly. This point is clarified in the following hadith:

> The Messenger of God (SAW) once met Gabriel[24] and said to him, "O Gabriel, I have been sent to an unlettered people, some of whom are frail and elderly, some of whom are mere youths, some of whom are servant women, and some of whom are men who have never read a book in their entire lives." "O Muhammad," Gabriel replied, "The Qur'an was revealed with seven pronunciations" (or "in seven dialects": literally, "on seven letters" – *ʿalā sabʿati aḥruf*) [and in another different wording:] "So let them recite it with any of these seven."[25]

The Open Language and Scientific Discoveries

The innumerable discoveries being made today of the Qur'an's miraculous insights into matters pertaining to scientific knowledge have to do with facts previously unknown to humankind and which, for this reason, have remained concealed for long centuries beneath the wings of this open and multifaceted language of which we speak. Note discoveries such as these are simply one fruit of this particular linguistic feature of the divine Revelation, and we owe a debt to the farsighted vision of the noble Companions who preserved the Qur'an without allowing interpretations of it to be recorded for posterity.

Those following them however (commentators, then translators) tried to decipher or explain what was clearly beyond their comprehension, going on to distort in the process, without meaning to, people's understanding of the Qur'an. The following discussion focuses on one such example, among many:

وَتَرَى الْجِبَالَ تَحْسَبُهَا جَامِدَةً وَهِيَ تَمُرُّ مَرَّ السَّحَابِ صُنْعَ اللَّهِ الَّذِي أَتْقَنَ كُلَّ شَيْءٍ إِنَّهُ خَبِيرٌ بِمَا تَفْعَلُونَ.

Wa tarā [And you see] *al-jibāla* [the mountains] *taḥsabuhā* [you think them] *jāmidatan* [stationary] *wa hiya* [while they are] *tamurru* [moving] *marra* [as the movement of] *al-saḥāb* [the clouds], *ṣunᶜa Allāh* [a work of God] *alladhī atqana* [Who has perfected] *kulla shayin* [all things]. *Innahu* [Lo!] *khabīrun* [He is Informed] *bimā* [of what] *tafᶜalūn* [ye do]. (*Sūrah al-Anᶜām* 27:88)

When I first pondered this verse, I was astounded at the clarity with which it affirms that the mountains 'rotate' along with the rotation of the Earth, just as clouds move across the sky. In thinking about this, it occurred to me to return to early commentaries on this verse to see how their authors understood it in the light of their eras' limited knowledge of the Earth and its relationship to the wider universe. At that time, no one as yet knew of the Earth's rotation or even that it was a sphere. In addition it is only relatively recently that geologists have learned that the Earth consists of layers, two of which are the crust (thin, in comparison to other layers, outermost layer) and the mantle (dense layer underneath the crust). According to the theory of plate tectonics, the Earth's crust moves over the mantle a few centimeters each year causing continents to drift (see Alfred Wegener's theory of continental drift which was proposed only in 1912, and interestingly deeply criticised by scientists until the 1950s when after his death evidence finally supported his discovery).

The following summarises attempts to interpret verse 27:88 by some of the most prominent early commentators of the Qur'an:

- **Al-Khāzin**: "The mountains move like clouds until they fall onto the Earth and are flattened...Similarly, the movement of the mountains on the Day of Resurrection will not be perceptible owing to their immense size, just as the movement of the clouds cannot be perceived for the same reason."
- **Al-Ṭabarī** [along with al-Nasafī, Ibn al-Jawzī, al-Zamakhsharī and al-Qurṭubī]: "Ibn ʿAbbās is reported to have said that the word *jāmidah* in this verse means 'firm' or 'standing upright'. As for the phrase, *wa hiya tamurru marra al-saḥāb*, it means that the mountains are to be gathered together [on Judgement Day], then caused to move such that someone who sees them will, owing to their great number, think they are standing still even as they hasten onward."
- **Al-Rāzī** [in agreement with al-Bayḍawī]: "The reason the mountains are to be perceived [on Judgement Day] as being *jāmidah* [rendered by Asad as 'so firm'] is that when large bodies move rapidly and in unison, those who look at them will think that are standing still even though they are passing by with great rapidity."
- **Abū Ḥayyān**: "It has been said that the reason why the person who looks at the mountains will think they are 'firm' (*jāmidah*), although they are moving, is that [his perception will be altered by] the frightening momentousness of that day [the Day of

Judgment]. In other words, he will not have the presence of mind to determine with certainty that they are not, in fact, standing still."

- **Ibn Kathīr**: "That is, you will see them as though they are stationary and unchanging when, in fact, they are passing by like clouds, that is, being removed from their place."
- **Al-Farrā'** [along with al-Akhfash al Awsaṭ]: These commentators provide no explanation of the verse.

What is most disturbing is that even some modern interpreters of the Qur'an insist on stopping at the point reached centuries ago by early scholars, content with the interpretations their extremely limited knowledge had caused them to reach. For example, if we take a selection of ten modern English commentaries on the Qur'an (eight written by Muslims and two by non-Muslim Orientalists), we find that all the eight commentaries by Muslims (or, rather, their translations of Arabic commentaries) cling tenaciously to interpretations produced by early commentators.

As a result, the phrase *wa hiya tamurru marra al-saḥāb* (while they are moving, or passing, as the movement of the clouds) has not been left as it is. In its interpretation, it has been considered necessary to transpose it into the future, a step that renders its actual meaning completely inaccessible to the English reader. Nevertheless, each of the translations insists on causing the verse to read, "will pass away" instead of: They are passing or moving.

Looking at this example further, even modern translators of the Qur'an have fallen into a peculiar and astonishing contradiction by translating the verb in the phrase *taḥsabuhā* (you deem them, think them to be) with the future tense instead of the present tense. The verb phrase *taḥsabuhā* refers to a present action, not a future one so has no meaning if it is rendered in the future tense. Nevertheless, most modern translations agree in rendering this verb in the future tense. Some translations (cf Hilali and Khan), in attempting to avoid the resulting contradiction, distort the meaning of the verse even further by rendering both this phrase (*taḥsabuhā*) and the adverbial phrase following it (*wa hiya tamurru marra al-saḥāb*) in the future tense: "And you will see the mountains and think them solid, but they shall pass away as the passing away of the clouds" [emphasis added].

Fortunately, the non-Muslim, British Orientalist Richard Bell was free from the influence of early commentators when he undertook his translation of the Qur'an (completed 1937–1939). He looked at the text, if not with an eye for modernity, then, at least, with an eye for the rules of Arabic grammar. Therefore, placing only these rules before him, he translated this verse using the present rather than the future tense and thus produced a precise, accurate rendering as follows: "*And one sees the mountains apparently solid, yet passing like clouds.*"

Richard Bell was followed by the Muslim translator, Muhammad Marmaduke Pickthall, whose English rendering of the Qur'an was first published in 1930 (though the revised edition published in 2002 has been chosen for this sample). Pickthall translates the verse as follows: "*And you see the hills [and] you deem them solid while they are flying the flight of clouds.*"

In sum, the above example presents us with a clear picture of how a remarkable, miraculous aspect of the Qur'an continued to be obscured, rather than revealed, when some of its translators into English decided to imitate the interpretations of centuries old commentators seemingly oblivious to the fact that they had based their understanding on the limited knowledge available to them during their lifetimes.

Lastly, I must confess that, as I come to the end of my first journey in the study of the miraculous innovations in the language of the Qur'an, it has been a human "adventure" of discovery which, like all human endeavors, remains weak and inadequate no matter how scientific, academic or objective it may aspire to be. No human attempt to treat the divine language of the Qur'an will ever merit being described as more than an "adventure." How much weaker and more inadequate will such an attempt be when its subject matter is the perfect divine expression that suffers no lack or weakness of any sort, and which is untainted by even a shadow of error or falsehood?

The divine challenge to the Arabs of the Prophet's day to "...produce a *sūrah* of similar merit,..." (Asad), or "...produce a Sūra like thereunto..." (Abdullah Yusuf Ali) (*Sūrah al-Baqarah* 2:23) still stands as though the Qur'an had been revealed only yesterday. Whatever geniuses have graced the world down the ages, nothing and no one has succeeded in detracting from its imposing stature.

NOTES

1 Fakhr al-Dīn al-Rāzī, *Al-Tafsīr al-Kabīr* (Beirut: Dār Iḥyā' al-Turāth al-ʿArabī, 2001), Part 9, p. 446.

2 Jalāl al-Dīn al-Suyūṭī, *Al-Itqān fī ʿUlūm al-Qur'ān* (Beirut: Dār al-Kutub al-ʿIlmiyyah, 2003), Part 2, p. 108.

3 *Sūrah al-Naḥl* 16:60, A.J. Arberry, *The Koran Interpreted* (New York: Macmillan, 1955).

4 This account was narrated by al-Ḥākim in *al-Mustadrak ʿalā al-Ṣaḥīḥayn*. Other accounts of stances taken by polytheists toward the Qur'an are mentioned by Samirah al-Zayid in *Mukhtaṣar al-Jāmiʿ fī al-Sīrah al-Nabawiyyah* (Damascus: Al-Maṭbaʿah al-ʿIlmiyyah, 1995).

5 In my documentation of pre-Islamic poetry, I have relied for the most part on the encyclopedia of poetry (on CD) compiled by the United Arab Emirates cultural academy. This encyclopedia has been issued in several editions. The first edition was published in 1998, the second in 2000, and the third in 2003. For the record, I should state here that without this encyclopedia in particular, as well as other also available on CD, I would not have been able to complete my research on this topic.

6 This instance occurs in the declaration that *wa lam yakun lahu kufuwan aḥad*, which is rendered as, "there is nothing that could be compared with Him" (*Sūrah al-Ikhlāṣ* 112:4). The negative verb phrase *lam yakun*, translated as "there is nothing," actually means "there was nothing, there is nothing, and never will be anything." Hence, its meaning is not limited to the past alone as it would be in human usages of this verb.

7 Narrated on the authority of Saʿd ibn Abī Waqqāṣ, *Siyar Aʿlām al-Nubalā*, al-Dhahabi.

8 The authors of these statements are: (1) Ibn al-Muqaffaʿ, *Kalīlah wa Dimnah*, p. 68; (2) Ibn Ḥazm, *Ṭawq al-Ḥamāmah*, p. 216; (3) Taha Husayn, *Fī al-Adab al-Jāhilī*, p. 315; (4) Al-Maʿarrī, *Rasā'il Abī al-ʿAlā' al-Maʿarrī*, vol. 3, p. 587; and (5) Al-Rafii, *Waḥi al-Qalam*, vol. 1, p. 16.

9 The art of reciting the Qur'an in keeping with established rules of pronunciation and intonation.

10 Jeffrey Lang, *Even Angels Ask: A Journey to Islam in America* (Beltsville, MA: Amana Publications, 1997), p. 139. The Arberry quote is taken from Arthur J. Arberry, *The Koran Interpreted* (Oxford: Oxford University Press, 1964), Introduction. The Denny quote is taken from Fredrick Denny, *Islam* (New York: Harper & Row Publishers, 1987), p. 88.

11 Abū Zakariyyā Yaḥyā ibn Sharaf al-Nawawī, *Riyāḍ al-Ṣāliḥīn*, ed. Abd al-Aziz Rabah and Ahmad Yusuf al-Daqqaq, (Damascus: Dār al-Ma'mūn li al-Turāth, 1980), p. 4.

12 Narrated by Aḥmad (Aḥmad ibn Ḥanbal, *Musnad*).

13 In this verse I depart from the translations (interpretations) of both Muhammad Asad and Abdullah Yusuf Ali.

14 Christoph Luxenberg, *The Syro-Aramaic Reading of the Koran: A Contribution to the Decoding of the Language of the Koran* (Berlin: Verlag Hans Schiller, 2007).

15 An example of a *ḥarf maṣdarī* would be the particle *an*, which can be followed either by the subjunctive (*naṣb*) in the present tense, or by a verb in the past tense. One might say, "after he went" (*baᶜda an dhahaba*) or "after he goes" (*baᶜda an yadhhaba*). Either of these combinations of the particle *an* with a following verb can be substituted with a verbal noun (*maṣdar*). Hence, instead of saying *baᶜda an dhahaba*, "after he went," one could say, *baᶜda dhahābihi* (literally, "after his going"), and instead of *baᶜda an yadhhaba*, "after he goes," one could also say, *baᶜda dhahābihi* (literally, "after his going").

16 Asad translates the phrase as, "God caused it to taste the all-embracing misery of hunger and fear," referring in a footnote to the way in which misfortune "envelops man like a garment" (*Tāj al-ᶜArūs*). See Muhammad Asad, *The Message of the Qur'ān* (Gibraltar: Dar al-Andalus, 1984), p. 414.

17 Al-Shawkānī, *Tafsīr Fatḥ al-Qadīr* (Cairo: Dār al-Fikr, no date), vol. 3, p. 200.

18 Al-Sakkākī, *Miftāh al-ᶜUlūm* (Beirut: Dār al-Kutub al-ᶜIlmiyyah, 2000), p. 298.

19 Narrated by al-Ḥākim. For a number of related accounts about ᶜUmar, see Jalāl al-Dīn al-Suyūṭī, *Jāmiᶜ al-Aḥādīth li al-Masānīd wa al-Marāsīl*, compiled and arranged by Ahmad Abd al-Jawwad and Abbas Ahmad Saqr (Damascus: Maṭbaᶜat Muḥammad Hāshim al-Kutubī, 1981); section on *masānīd* (plural of *musnad*, a tradition traceable in uninterrupted ascending order to its first authority), vol. 2, pp. 143-145.

20 The Arabic translation is taken from the edition published by Dār al-Kitāb al-Muqaddas fī al-ᶜĀlam al-ᶜArabī, 1981.

21 Dār al-Kitāb al-Muqaddas fī al-ᶜĀlam al-ᶜArabī, edition 2004.

22 See Ahmad Ali al-Imam, *Variant Readings of the Qur'an: A Critical Study of Their Historical and Linguistic Origins* (Malta: IIIT, 2011).

23 Narrated by both al-Bukhārī and Muslim with some difference in wording. For more hadiths on this topic, see books written on the subject of the Qur'an's variant readings, especially the introduction to Ibn al-Jazarī (d. 833 AH/1429 CE), *Taqrīb al-Nashr fī al-Qirā'āt al-ᶜAshr*, ed. Ibrahim Atwah Awad, (Cairo: Dār al-Ḥadīth, 1966), pp. 47-51.

24 One version of this account mentions that he met Gabriel "at the rocks of al-Marā'," which is a reference to a mountain in Qubā'.

25 Narrated by al-Tirmidhī on the authority of Ubayy ibn Kaᶜb.

SELECTED SOURCES AND REFERENCES

The following listing does not include hadith collections, dictionaries, encyclopedias, works on grammar and language, or Qur'anic commentaries to which we have not made reference in this study. Nor does it include the numerous encyclopedias in CD form on which we have relied, including encyclopedias of the Holy Qur'an, Prophetic Hadith, and Arabic poetry, particularly the 1998, 2000 and 2003 editions of the important encyclopedia (on CD) compiled by the United Arab Emirates cultural academy.

Arabic Language Sources

Alalwani, Taha Jabir. *Naḥwa Mawqif Qur'ānī min al-Naskh* (Cairo: Maktabat al-Shurūq al-Dawliyah, 2007).

Al-Ansari, Ahmad Makki. *Naẓariyyat al-Naḥw al-Qur'ānī* (Jeddah: Dār al-Qiblah, 1405 AH/1984 CE).

Al-Aṣbahānī, Abū Bakr Aḥmad ibn al-Ḥusayn. *Al-Mabsūṭ fī al-Qirā'āt al-ʿAshar*, ed. Subai Hamzah Hakimi, (Jeddah: Dār al-Qiblah and Beirut: Mu'assasat ʿUlūm al-Qur'ān, 1995).

Al-Bāqillānī, al-Qāḍī Abū Bakr Muḥammad ibn al-Ṭayyib. *Iʿjāz al-Qur'ān*. Edited and Annotated by Salah ibn Uwaydah, (Beirut: Dār al-Kutub al-ʿIlmiyyah, 2001).

Al-Farāhī, ʿAbd al-Ḥamīd. *Tafsīr Niẓām al-Qur'ān wa Ta'wīl al-Furqān bil-Furqān* (India: Al-Dā'irah al-Ḥamidiyyah, 2000).

Ibn al-Jazarī, Muḥammad ibn Muḥammad. *Taqrīb al-Nashr fī al-Qirā'āt al-ʿAshr*, ed. Ibrahim Atwah Awad, (Cairo: Dār al-Ḥadīth, 1996).

Al-Jurjānī, ʿAbd al-Qāhir. *Dalā'il al-Iʿjāz*, with commentary by Mahmud Muhammad Shakir, (Cairo and Jeddah: Dār al-Madanī, 1992).

Al-Kitāb al-Muqaddas (Beirut: Dār al-Kitāb al-Muqaddas fī al-Sharq al-Awsaṭ, 2004).

Al-Kitāb al-Muqaddas (Dār al-Kitāb al-Muqaddas fī al-ʿĀlam al-ʿArabī, 1981).

Al-Qaṭṭān, Manāʿ. *Mabāḥith fī ʿUlūm al-Qur'ān* (Beirut: Mu'assasat al-Risālah, 1998).

Al-Rāzī, al-Fakhr. *Al-Tafsīr al-Kabīr* (Beirut: Dār Iḥyā' al-Turāth al-ʿArabī, 2001).

Al-Sakākī, Abū Yaʿqūb Yūsuf. *Miftāḥ al-ʿUlūm*, ed. ʿAbd al-Hamid Hindawi, (Beirut: Dār al-Kutub al-ʿIlmiyah, 2000).

Al-Shawkānī, Muḥammad ibn ʿAlī. *Fatḥ al-Qadīr: al-Jāmiʿ bayn Fannay al-Riwāyah wa al-Dirāyah min ʿIlm al-Tafsīr* (Cairo: Dār al-Fikr, no date).

Al-Suyūṭī, Jalāl al-Dīn. *Al-Itqān fī ʿUlūm al-Qur'ān*, ed. Muhammad Salim Hashim, (Beirut: Dār al-Kutub al-ʿIlmiyyah, 2003).

__________. *Jāmiʿ al-Aḥādīth li al-Masānīd wa al-Marāsīl*. Compiled and arranged by Ahmad Abd al-Jawwad and Abbas Ahmad Saqr, (Damascus: Maṭbaʿat Muḥammad Hāshim al-Kutubī, 1981).

Udaymah, Muhammad Abd al-Khaliq. *Dirāsāt li Uslūb al-Qur'ān al-Karīm* (Cairo: Dār al-Ḥadīth, 2004).

Al-Zarkashī, Badr al-Dīn Muḥammad ibn Bahādir. *Al-Burhān fī ʿUlūm al-Qur'ān*, ed. Muhammad Abu al-Fadl Ibrahim, (Cairo: Dār Iḥyā' al-Kutub al-ʿArabiyah, 1958).

Al-Zayid, Samirah. *Mukhtaṣar al-Jāmiʿ fī al-Sīrah al-Nabawiyyah* (Damascus: Al-Maṭbaʿah al-ʿIlmiyyah, 1995).

English Language Sources

Asad, Muhammad. *The Message of the Qur'ān* (Bristol, England: The Book Foundation, 2003), vol. 5.

The Bible. King James Version (London: Collins' Clear-Type Press, 1950).

Good News for Modern Man: The New Testament in Today's English Version (American Bible Society, 1966).

The Holy Bible. Revised Standard Version (Division of Christian Education of the National Council of the Churches of Christ in the U.S.A. Great Britain, 1971).

The Holy Bible (London: Trinitarian Bible Society, 2000).

Islahi, Amin Ahsan. *Pondering over the Qur'an*, trans. M. S. Kayani. (London, 2003).

Lang, Jeffrey. *Even Angels Ask: A Journey to Islam in America* (Beltsville, MA: Amana Publications, 1997).

Luxenberg, Christoph. *The Syro-Aramaic Reading of the Koran: A Contribution to the Decoding of the Language of the Koran*. English Edition. (Germany, 2007).

Murry, Middleton. *The Problem of Style* (1922) (London: Oxford Paperbacks, 1960).